The Letters of Lord Nelson to Lady Hamilton

By Horatio Nelson
Cover Design by Alex Struik

Copyright © 2012 Alex Struik.

Alex Struik retains sole copyright to the cover design of this edition of this book.

All rights reserved. No part of this publication may be reproduced, stored in a retrieval system, or transmitted, in any form or by any means, electronic, mechanical, photocopying, recording or otherwise, without the prior permission of the copyright owner.

The right of Alex Struik to be identified as the author of the cover design of this work has been asserted in accordance with the Copyright, Designs and Patents Act 1988.

ISBN-13: 978-1480051881

ISBN-10: 1480051888

Contents

LETTER I.	10
LETTER II.	12
LETTER III.	13
LETTER IV.	14
LETTER V.	15
LETTER VI.	16
LETTER VII.	18
LETTER VIII.	19
LETTER IX.	21
LETTER X.	24
LETTER XI.	27
LETTER XII.	28
LETTER XIII.	31
LETTER XIV.	34
LETTER XV.	36
LETTER XVI.	39
LETTER XVII.	42
LETTER XVIII.	43
LETTER XIX.	46
LETTER XX.	48
LETTER XXI.	51
LETTER XXII.	53
LETTER XXIII.	56
LETTER XXIV.	57
LETTER XXV.	60

LETTER XXVI. 61
LETTER XXVII. 62
LETTER XXVIII. 65
LETTER XXIX. 68
LETTER XXX. 70
LETTER XXXI. 73
LETTER XXXII. 76
LETTER XXXIII. 82
LETTER XXXIV. 85
LETTER XXXV. 87
LETTER XXXVI. 88
LETTER XXXVII. 94
LETTER XXXVIII. 96
LETTER XXXIX. 97
LETTER XL. 104
LETTER XLI. 107
LETTER XLII. 112
LETTER XLIII. 115
LETTER XLIV. 117
LETTER XLV. 120
LETTER XLVI. 121
LETTER XLVII. 123
LETTER XLVIII. 128
LETTER XLIX. 131
LETTER L. 133
LETTER LI. 136
LETTER LII. 138

LETTER LIII. 139

LETTER LIV. 142

LETTER LV. 144

LETTER LVI. 145

LETTER LVII. 147

LETTER LVIII. 149

LETTER LIX. 153

LETTER LX. 155

SUPPLEMENT 157

LETTERS FROM LORD NELSON,TO MISS HORATIA NELSON THOMSON,NOW MISS HORATIA NELSON, (Lord Nelson's Adopted Daughter;) AND MISS CHARLOTTE NELSON, (Daughter of the present Earl.) 157

LETTERS FROM ALEXANDER DAVISON, ESQ. TO LADY HAMILTON. 159

    I. 159

    II. 161

    III. 163

Letter from Lady Hamilton TO ALEXANDER DAVISON, ESQ. INCLOSING Her Ladyship's Verses on Lord Nelson. 165

Letter from Lady Hamilton TO THE RIGHT HONOURABLE HENRY ADDINGTON, NOW VISCOUNT SIDMOUTH. 168

Letters FROM SIR WILLIAM HAMILTON, K.B. TO LADY HAMILTON. 170

    I. 170

    II. 172

III.	174
IV.	176
V.	178
VI.	179
VII.	180
VIII.	182
IX.	184
X.	186
XI.	187
XII.	189
XIII.	191
XIV.	192
XV.	194
XVI.	196
XVII.	198
Letters FROM SIR WILLIAM HAMILTON, K.B. TO LORD NELSON.	**199**
I.	199
II.	202
III.	203
IV.	204
V.	206
VI.	207
VII.	208
VIII.	211
IX.	212
X.	214

XI. 217

XII. 219

Letters FROM LORD NELSON TO SIR WILLIAM
HAMILTON, K.B. 221

I. 221

II. 222

III. 224

IV. 227

V. 228

VI. 230

VII. 231

VIII. 232

IX. 235

X. 236

XI. 237

XII. 239

Letters FROM LORD NELSON TO MRS. THOMSON.
....241

I. 241

II. 242

Letters FROM LADY HAMILTON TO LORD NELSON.
....244

I. 244

II. 246

Letters FROM THE REV. EDMUND NELSON (Lord
Nelson's Father) TO LADY HAMILTON. 247

I. 247

II. 248

Letters From The REV. DR. NELSON, NOW EARL NELSON, TO LADY HAMILTON. 249
    I. 249
    II. 251
    III. 253
    IV. 255
    V. 257
    VI. 259

Letters FROM THE EARL OF ST. VINCENT TO LADY HAMILTON. 260
    I. 260
    II. 261
    III. 263
    IV. 265
    V. 266

Letters FROM SIR ALEXANDER JOHN BALL TO LADY HAMILTON. 268
    I. 268
    II. 270

Letters FROM THE EARL OF BRISTOL, Bishop of Derry, in Ireland, TO LADY HAMILTON. 271
    I. 271
    II. 272
    III. 273
    IV. 274
    V. 275
    VI. 276
    VII. 277

VIII.	278
IX.	279
X.	280

Letter FROM THE HONOURABLE CHARLES GREVILLE, Nephew of Sir William Hamilton, TO LADY HAMILTON. 283

FROM LADY HAMILTON TO THE HON. CHARLES GREVILLE, Nephew of Sir William Hamilton. 284

I.	284
II.	286

LETTER I.

Vanguard, off Malta,
Oct. 24, 1798.

MY DEAR MADAM,

After a long passage, we are arrived; and it is as I suspected—the ministers at Naples know nothing of the situation of the island. Not a house or bastion of the town is in possession of the islanders; and the Marquis de Niza tells me, they want arms, victuals, and support. He does not know, that any Neapolitan officers are in the island; perhaps, although I have their names, none are arrived; and it is very certain, by the Marquis's account, that no supplies have been sent by the governors of Syracuse or Messina.

However, I shall and will know every thing as soon as the Marquis is gone, which will be to-morrow morning. He says, he is very anxious to serve under my command; and, by his changing his ship, it appears as if he was so: however, I understand the trim of our English ships better.

Ball will have the management of the blockade after my departure; as, it seems, the Court of Naples think my presence may be necessary, and useful, in the beginning of November.

I hope it will prove so; but, I feel, my duty lays at present in the East; for, until I know the shipping in Egypt are destroyed, I shall never consider the French army as completely sure of never returning to Europe.

However, all my views are to serve and save the Two Sicilies; and to do that which their Majesties may wish me, even against my own opinion, when I come to Naples, and that country is at war. I shall wish to have a meeting with General Acton on this subject.

You will, I am sure, do me justice with the Queen; for, I declare to
God, my whole study is, how to best meet her approbation.

May God bless you and Sir William! and ever believe me, with the most affectionate regard, your obliged and faithful friend,

HORATIO NELSON.

I may possibly, but that is not certain, send in the inclosed letter.
Shew it to Sir William. This must depend on what I hear and see; for
I believe scarcely any thing I hear.

Once more, God bless you!

LETTER II.

[May 12, 1799.]

MY DEAR LADY HAMILTON,

Accept my sincere thanks for your kind letter. Nobody writes so well: therefore, pray, say not you write ill; for, if you do, I will say—what your goodness sometimes told me—"You l—e!" I can read, and perfectly understand, every word you write.

We drank your and Sir William's health. Troubridge, Louis, Hallowell, and the new Portuguese Captain, dined here. I shall soon be at Palermo; for this business must very soon be settled.

No one, believe me, is more sensible of your regard, than your obliged and grateful

NELSON.

I am pleased with little Mary; kiss her for me. I thank all the house for their regard. God bless you all!

I shall send on shore, if fine, to-morrow; for the feluccas are going to leave us, and I am sea-sick.

I have got the piece of wood for the tea-chest; it shall soon be sent.

Pray, present my humble duty and gratitude to the Queen, for all her marks of regard; and assure her, it is not thrown away on an ungrateful soil.

LETTER III.

Vanguard, May 19, 1799,
Eight o'Clock. Calm.

MY DEAR LADY HAMILTON,

Lieutenant Swiney coming on board, enables me to send some blank passports for vessels going to Procida with corn, &c. and also one for the courier boat.

To tell you, how dreary and uncomfortable the Vanguard appears, is only telling you, what it is to go from the pleasantest society to a solitary cell; or, from the dearest friends, to no friends. I am now perfectly the great man—not a creature near me. From my heart, I wish myself the little man again!

You, and good Sir William, have spoiled me for any place but with you. I love Mrs. Cadogan. You cannot conceive what I feel, when I call you all to my remembrance. Even to Mira, do not forget your faithful and affectionate

NELSON.

LETTER IV.

May 20, 1799.

MY DEAR LADY HAMILTON,

Many thanks to you and Sir William for your kind notes. You will believe I did not sleep much, with all my letters to read, &c. &c.

My letters from Lord St. Vincent are May 6th. He says—"We saw the Brest squadron pass us yesterday, under an easy sail. I am making every effort to get information to Lord Keith; who I have ordered here, to complete their water and provisions. I conjecture, the French squadron is bound for Malta and Alexandria, and the Spanish fleet for the attack of Minorca."

I must leave you to judge, whether the Earl will come to us. I think he will: but, entre nous, Mr. Duckworth means to leave me to my fate. I send you (under all circumstances) his letter. Never mind; if I can get my eleven sail together, they shall not hurt me.

God bless you, Sir William, and all our joint friends in your house; Noble, Gibbs, &c. and believe me ever, for ever, your affectionate friend,

NELSON.

LETTER V.

February 3, 1800.

MY DEAR LADY HAMILTON,

Having a Commander in Chief, I cannot come on shore till I have made my manners to him. Times are changed; but, if he does not come on shore directly, I will not wait.

In the mean time, I send Allen to inquire how you are. Send me word, for I am anxious to hear of you. It has been no fault of mine, that I have been so long absent. I cannot command; and, now, only obey.

Mr. Tyson, and the Consul, have not been able to find out the betrothed wife of the Priore; although they were three days in their inquiries, and desired the Neapolitan Consul to send to Pisa. I also desired the Russian Admiral, as he was going to Pisa, to inquire if the Countess Pouschkin had any letters to send to Palermo; but, as I received none, I take for granted she had none to send.

May God bless you, my dear Lady; and be assured, I ever am, and shall be, your obliged and affectionate

BRONTE NELSON.

LETTER VI.

Off La Valette, Feb. 20, 1800.

MY DEAR LADY HAMILTON,

Had you seen the Peer receive me, I know not what you would have done; but, I can guess. But never mind! I told him, that I had made a vow, if I took the Genereux by myself, it was my intention to strike my flag. To which he made no answer.

If I am well enough, I intend to write a letter to Prince Leopold, and to send him the French Admiral's flag; which I hope you will approve of, as it was taken on the coast of his father's kingdom, and by as faithful a subject as any in his dominions.

I have had no communication with the shore; therefore, have seen neither Ball, Troubridge, or Graham: nor with the Lion; when I have, I shall not forget all your messages, and little Jack. I only want to know your wishes, that I may, at least, appear grateful, by attending to them.

My head aches dreadfully, and I have none here to give me a moment's comfort.

I send the packet to General Acton; as I think it may go quicker, and he will be flattered by presenting the flag and letter to the Prince.

Malta, I think, will fall very soon, if these other corvettes do not get in.

Pray, make my best regards acceptable to Mrs. Cadogan, Miss Knight, little Mary Re Giovanni, Gibbs, &c. &c. and ever believe me your truly faithful and affectionate

 BRONTE NELSON.

LETTER VII.

June 16, [1800.] Seven o'Clock.

MY DEAR LADY HAMILTON,

What a difference—but it was to be—from your house to a boat!

Fresh breeze of wind, the ship four or five leagues from the mole; getting on board into truly a hog-stye of a cabin, leaking like a sieve, consequently floating with water. What a change!

Not a felucca near us. I saw them come out this morning, but they think there is too much wind and swell.

Pray, do not keep the cutter; as I have not a thing, if any thing important should arrive, to send you.

Only think of Tyson's being left!

May God bless you, my dear Lady; and believe me, ever, your truly affectionate and sincere friend,

NELSON.

Lady Hamilton—Put the candlestick on my writing-table.

LETTER VIII.

January 28, 1801.

What a fool I was, my dear Lady Hamilton, to direct that your cheering letters should be directed for Brixham! I feel, this day, truly miserable, in not having them; and, I fear, they will not come till to-morrow's post.

What a blockhead, to believe any person is so active as myself! I have this day got my orders, to put myself under Lord St. Vincent's command: but, as no order is arrived to man the ship, it must be Friday night, or Saturday morning, before she can sail for Torbay. Direct my letters, now, to Brixham.

My eye is very bad. I have had the physician of the fleet to examine it.

He has directed me not to write, (and yet I am forced, this day, to write Lord Spencer, St. Vincent, Davison about my law-suit, Troubridge, Mr. Locker, &c. but you are the only female I write to;) not to eat any thing but the most simple food; not to touch wine or porter; to sit in a dark room; to have green shades for my eyes—(will you, my dear friend, make me one or two? Nobody else shall;)—and to bathe them in cold water every hour. I fear, it is the writing has brought on this complaint. My eye is like blood; and the film so extended, that I only see from the corner farthest from my nose. What a fuss about my complaints! But, being so far from my sincere friends, I have leisure to brood over them.

I have this moment seen Mrs. Thomson's friend. Poor fellow! he seems very uneasy and melancholy. He begs you to be kind to her; and I have assured him of your readiness to relieve the dear good woman: and believe me, for ever, my dear Lady, your faithful, attached, and affectionate,

NELSON & BRONTE.

I will try and write the Duke a line. My brother intended to have gone off to-morrow afternoon; but this half order may stop him.

LETTER IX.

San Josef, February 8th, 1801.

MY DEAR LADY,

Mr. Davison demands the privilege of carrying back an answer to your kind letter; and, I am sure, he will be very punctual in the delivery.

I am not in very good spirits; and, except that our country demands all our services and abilities, to bring about an honourable peace, nothing should prevent my being the bearer of my own letter. But, my dear friend, I know you are so true and loyal an Englishwoman, that you would hate those who would not stand forth in defence of our King, laws, religion, and all that is dear to us.

It is your sex that make us go forth; and seem to tell us— "None but the brave deserve the fair!" and, if we fall, we still live in the hearts of those females. You are dear to us. It is your sex that rewards us; it is your sex who cherish our memories; and you, my dear, honoured friend, are, believe me, the first, the best, of your sex.

I have been the world around, and in every corner of it, and never yet saw your equal, or even one which could be put in comparison with you. You know how to reward virtue, honour, and courage; and never to ask if it is placed in a Prince, Duke, Lord, or Peasant: and I hope, one day, to see you, in peace, before I set out for Bronte, which I am resolved to do.

Darby's is one of the ships sent out after the French squadron; I shall, therefore, give the print to Hardy. I think, they might come by the mail-coach, as a parcel, wrapped up round a stick; any print shop will give you one: and direct it as my letters. The coach stops, for parcels, at the White Bear, I believe, Piccadilly.

Pray, have you got any picture from Mrs. Head's? I hope, Mr. Brydon has executed the frames to your satisfaction; the bill, he is directed to send to me.

Only tell me, how I can be useful to you and Sir William; and believe, nothing could give me more pleasure: being, with the greatest truth, my dear Lady, your most obliged and affectionate friend,

NELSON & BRONTE.

I am told, the moment St. George arrives, that I am to be tumbled out of this ship; as the Ville de Paris is going to Plymouth, to be paid, and the Earl will hoist his flag here: and if I am as fortunate in getting a fresh-painted cabin, (which is probable) I shall be knocked up. At all events, I shall be made very uncomfortable by this hurry.

It has been very good, and friendly, of Mr. Davison, to travel upwards of two hundred miles, to make me a visit.

I rather think, the great Earl will not much like his not having called on him; but his manner of speaking of Mr. Davison, for his friendship to me, in the matter of the law-suit, Lord St. Vincent states to my solicitors as offensive to him. Why should it? only that Mr. Davison wishes that I should have justice done me, and not to be overpowered by weight of interest and money.

Once more, God bless you and Sir William.

N. & B.

Sir Isaac Heard has gazetted Troubridge's, Hood, &c.'s honours; but has not gazetted mine: and he has the King's orders for mine as much as the others.

LETTER X.

No 2. San Josef, February 16th, 1801.

MY DEAREST FRIEND,

Your letters have made me happy, to-day; and never again will I scold, unless you begin. Therefore, pray, never do; My confidence in you is firm as a rock.

* * * * * * * * * * * * * *

I cannot imagine, who can have stopped my Sunday's letter! That it has been, is clear: and the seal of the other has been clearly opened; but this might have happened from letters sticking together.

Your's all came safe; but the numbering of them will point out, directly, if one is missing. I do not think, that any thing very particular was in that letter which is lost.

Believe me, my dear friend, that Lady A. is as damned a w—— as ever lived, and Mrs. W—— is a bawd! Mrs. U——— a foolish pimp; eat up with pride, that a P—— will condescend to put her to expence. Only do as I do; and all will be well, and you will be every thing I wish.

I thank you for your kindness to poor dear Mrs. Thomson. I send her a note; as desired by her dear good friend, who doats on her.

I send you a few Lines, wrote in the late gale; which, I think, you will not disapprove.

How interesting your letters are! You cannot write too much, or be too particular.

* * * * *

  Though ———'s polish'd verse superior shine,
  Though sensibility grace every line;
  Though her soft Muse be far above all praise.
  And female tenderness inspire her lays:

   Deign to receive, though unadorn'd
     By the poetic art,
   The rude expressions which bespeak
     A Sailor's untaught heart!

 A heart susceptible, sincere, and true;
 A heart, by fate, and nature, torn in two:
 One half, to duty and his country due;
 The other, better half, to love and you!

   Sooner shall Britain's sons resign
     The empire of the sea;
   Than Henry shall renounce his faith,
     AND PLIGHTED VOWS, TO THEE!

  And waves on wares shall cease to roll,
    And tides forget to flow;
  Ere thy true Henry's constant love,
    Or ebb, or change, shall know.

The weather, thank God, is moderating.

I have just got a letter from the new Earl at the Admiralty, full of compliments. But nothing shall stop my law-suit, and I hope to cast him.

I trust, when I get to Spithead, there will be no difficulty in getting leave of absence.

The letters on service are so numerous, from three days interruption of the post, that I must conclude with assuring you, that I am, for ever, your attached, and unalterably your's,

NELSON & BRONTE.

I shall begin a letter at night.

LETTER XI.

[March 1801.]

You say, my Dearest Friend, why don't I put my Chief forward? He has put me in the front of the battle, and Nelson will be first. I could say more; but will not make you uneasy, knowing the firm friendship you have for me.

The St. George will stamp an additional ray of glory to England's fame, if Nelson survives; and that Almighty Providence, who has hitherto protected me in all dangers, and covered my head in the day of battle, will still, if it be his pleasure, support and assist me.

Keep me alive, in your and Sir William's remembrance. My last thoughts will be with you both, for you love and esteem me. I judge your hearts by my own.

May the Great God of Heaven protect and bless you and him! is the fervent prayer of your and Sir William's unalterable friend, till death.

LETTER XII.

Friday Night, Nine o'Clock.
St. George. [March 1801.]

Having, my truly Dearest Friend, got through a great deal of business, I am enabled to do justice to my private feelings; which are fixed, ever, on you, and about you, whenever the public service does not arrest my attention.

I have read all, all, your kind and affectionate letters: and have read them frequently over; and committed them to the flames, much against my inclination. There was one I rejoiced not to have read at the time. It was, where you consented to dine and sing with * * * *. Thank God, it was not so! I could not have borne it; and, now, less than ever. But, I now know, he never can dine with you; for, you would go out of the house sooner than suffer it: and, as to letting him hear you sing, I only hope he will be struck deaf, and you dumb, sooner than such a thing should happen! But, I know, it never now can.

You cannot think how my feelings are alive towards you; probably, more than ever: and they never can be diminished. My hearty endeavours shall not be wanting, to improve and to give US NEW ties of regard and affection.

I have seen, and talked much with, Mrs. Thomson's friend. The fellow seems to eat all my words, when I talk of her and his child! He says, he never can forget your goodness and kind affection to her and his dear, dear child. I have had, you know, the felicity of seeing it, and a finer child never was produced by any two persons. It was, in truth, a love-begotten child! I am determined to keep him on board;

for, I know, if they got together, they would soon have another. But, after our two months trip, I hope, they will never be separated; and, then, let them do as they please.

We are all bustle and activity. I shall sail, on Monday, after your letter arrives. Troubridge will send it, as an Admiralty letter. On Tuesday I shall be in the Downs, if we have any wind; and Troubridge will send, under cover to Admiral Lutwidge.

It is not my intention to set my foot out of the ship, except to make my take-leave bow to Admiral Milbank. I have been much pressed to dine ashore: but, no; never, if I can help it, till I dine with you.

Eleven o'Clock.

Your dear letters just come on board. They are sympathetic with my own feelings; and, I trust, we shall soon meet, to part no more!

Monday, I shall be here for letters; Tuesday, at Deal. Recollect, I am, for ever, your's; aye, for ever, while life remains, your's, your's faithfully,

NELSON & BRONTE.

I charge my only friend to keep well, and think of her Nelson's glory.

I have written to Lord Eldon, the Chancellor, as my brother desired.

Pray, as you are going to buy a ticket for the Pigot diamond—buy the right number, or it will be money thrown away.

For ever, ever, your's, only your's.

Kindest regards to my dear Mrs. Thomson, and my God Child.

LETTER XIII.

Deal—[Shall be on board the Medusa before this letter go from the Downs]—July 31, 1801.

MY DEAREST EMMA,

Did not you get my letter from Sheerness on Thursday morning, telling you I was just setting off for Deal; as I have no letter from you of yesterday, only those of Wednesday, which went to Sheerness? It has been my damned blunder, and not your's; for which I am deservedly punished, by missing one of your dear letters. They are my comfort, joy, and delight.

My time is, truly, fully taken up, and my hand aches before night comes.

I got to bed, last night, at half past nine; but the hour was so unusual, that I heard the clock strike one. To say that I thought of you, would be nonsense; for, you are never out of my thoughts.

At this moment, I see no prospect of my getting to London; but, very soon, the business of my command will become so simple, that a child may direct it.

What rascals your post-chaise people must be! They have been paid
 every thing. Captain Parker has one receipt for seven pounds odd, and
 I am sure that every thing is paid; therefore, do not pay a farthing.
 The cart-chaise I paid at Dartford.

You need not fear all the women in this world; for all others, except yourself, are pests to me. I know but one; for, who can be like my Emma? I am confident, you will do nothing which can hurt my feelings; and I will die by torture, sooner than do any thing which could offend you.

Give ten thousand kisses to my dear Horatia.

Yesterday, the subject turned on the cow-pox. A gentleman declared, that his child was inoculated with the cow-pox; and afterwards remained in a house where a child had the small-pox the natural way, and did not catch it. Therefore, here was a full trial with the cow-pox. The child is only feverish for two days; and only a slight inflammation of the arm takes place, instead of being all over scabs. But, do you what you please!

I did not get your newspapers; therefore, do not know what promise you allude to: but this I know, I have none made me.

The extension of the patent of peerage is going on; but the wording of my brother's note, they have wrote for a meaning to. The patent must be a new creation. First, to my father, if he outlives me; then to William, and his sons; then to Mrs. Bolton, and her sons; and Mrs. Matcham, and her's. Farther than that, I care not; it is far enough. But it may never get to any of them; for the old patent may extend by issue male of my own carcase: I am not so very old; and may marry again, a wife more suitable to my genius.

I like the Morning Chronicle.

Ever, for ever, your's, only your,

NELSON & BRONTE.

Best regards to Mrs. Nelson, the Duke, and Lord William.

I have totally failed for poor Madame Brueys.

Bonaparte's wife is one of Martinique, and some plan is supposed to be carried on.

LETTER XIV.

Sheerness, August 11th, 1801.

MY DEAREST EMMA,

I came from Harwich yesterday noon; not having set my foot on shore, although the Volunteers, &c. were drawn up to receive me, and the people ready to draw the carriage.

Parker had very near got all the honours; but I want none, but what my dear Emma confers. You have sense to discriminate whether they are deserved or no.

I came on shore; for my business lays with the Admiral, who lives in a ship hauled on shore, and the Commisioner. Slept at Coffin's: and, having done all that I can, am off for the Downs; to-day, if possible.

As far as September 14th, I am at the Admiralty's disposal; but, if Mr. Buonaparte do not chuse to send his miscreants before that time. my health will not bear me through equinoctial gales.

I wish that Sir William was returned; I would try and persuade him to come to either Deal, Dover, or Margate: for, thus cut off from the society of my dearest friends, 'tis but a life of sorrow and sadness. But, patienza per forza!

I hope you will get the house. If I buy, no person can say—this shall, or not, be altered; and, you shall have the whole arrangement.

Remember me most kindly to Mrs. Nelson, the Duke, and Lord William.

Write to me in the Downs.

May the Heavens bless and preserve you, for ever and ever! is the constant prayer of, my dear Emma, your most affectionate and faithful

NELSON & BRONTE.

The Mayor and Corporation of Sandwich, when they came on board to present me the freedom of that ancient town, requested me [to] dine with them. I put them off for the moment, but they would not be let off. Therefore, this business, dreadful to me, stands over, and I shall be attacked again when I get to the Downs. But I will not dine there, without you say, approve; nor, perhaps, then, if I can get off. Oh! how I hate to be stared at.

LETTER XV.

Deal, August 18th, 1801.

MY DEAREST EMMA,

Your dear, good, kind, and most affectionate letters, from Saturday to last night, are arrived, and I feel all you say; and may Heaven bless me, very soon, with a sight of your dear angelic face. You are a nonpareil! No, not one fit to wipe your shoes. I am, ever have been, and always will remain, your most firm, fixed, and unalterable friend.

I wish Sir William had come home a week ago, then I should have seen you here.

I have this morning been attending the funeral of two young Mids: a Mr. Gore, cousin of Capt. Gore, and a Mr. Bristow. One nineteen, the other seventeen years of age.

Last night, I was all the evening in the Hospital, seeing that all was done for the comfort of the poor fellows.

I am going on board; for nothing should keep me living on shore, without you were here. I shall come in the morning, to see Parker, and go on board again directly.

I shall be glad to see Oliver: I hope he will keep his tongue quiet, about the tea-kettle; for, I shall not give it till I leave the Medusa.

You ask me, what Troubridge wrote me? There was not a syllable about you in it. It was about my not coming to London; at the importance of which, I laughed: and, then, he said, he should never venture another opinion. On which, I said—"Then, I shall never give you one." This day, he has wrote a kind letter, and all is over.

I have, however, wrote him, in my letter of this day, as follows—viz. "And I am, this moment, as firmly of opinion as ever, that Lord St. Vincent, and yourself, should have allowed of my coming to town, for my own affairs; for, every one knows, I left it without a thought for myself."

I know, he likes to be with you: but, shall he have that felicity, and he deprive me of it? No; that he shall not!

But this business cannot last long, and I hope we shall have peace; and, I rather incline to that opinion. But the Devil should not get me out of the kingdom, without being some days with you.

I hope, my dear Emma, you will be able to find a house suited for my comfort. I am sure of being HAPPY, by your arrangements.

I have wrote a line to Troubridge, about Darby.

Parker will write you a line of thanks, if he is able. I trust in God, he will yet do well!

You ask me, my dear friend, if I am going on more expeditions? And, even if I was to forfeit your friendship, which is dearer to me than all the world, I can tell you nothing.

For, I go out; [if] I see the enemy, and can get at them, it is my duty: and you would naturally hate me, if I kept back one moment.

I long to pay them, for their tricks t'other day, the debt of a drubbing, which, surely, I'll pay: but when, where, or how, it is impossible, your own good sense must tell you, for me or mortal man to say.

I shall act not in a rash or hasty manner; that you may rely, and on which I give you my word of honour.

Just going off. Ever, for ever, your faithful

NELSON & BRONTE.

Every kind thing to Mrs. Nelson.

LETTER XVI.

Medusa, Downs, August 31st, 1801.

MY DEAR EMMA! DEAREST, BEST, FRIEND OF NELSON,

Sir William is arrived, and well; remember me kindly to him. I should have had the pleasure of seeing him, but for one of my lords and masters, TROUBRIDGE; therefore, I am sure, neither you or Sir William will feel obliged to him.

The weather is very bad, and I am very sea-sick. I cannot answer your letter, probably; but I am writing a line, to get on shore, if possible: indeed, I hardly expect that your letter can get afloat.

I entreat you, my dear friend, to work hard for me, and get the house and furniture; and I will be so happy to lend it to you and Sir William!

Therefore, if you was to take the Duke's house, a cake house, open to every body he pleases, you had better have a booth at once; you never could rest one moment quiet. Why did not the Duke assist Sir William, when he wanted his assistance? why not have saved you from the distress, which Sir William must every day feel, in knowing that his excellent wife sold her jewels to get a house for him; whilst his own relations, great as they are in the foolish world's eye, would have left a man of his respectability and age, to have lodged in the streets. Did the Duke, or any of them, give him a house then?

Forgive me! you know if any thing sticks in my throat, it must out. Sir William owes his life to you; which, I believe, he will never forget.

To return to the house—The furniture must be bought with it; and the sooner it is done, the better I shall like it.

Oh! how bad the weather is!

The devils, here, wanted to plague my soul out, yesterday, just after dinner; but I would have seen them damned, before they should have come in. The Countess Montmorris, Lady this, that, and t'other, came along-side, a Mr. Lubbock with them—to desire they might come in. I sent word, I was so busy that no persons could be admitted, as my time was employed in the King's service. Then they sent their names, which I cared not for: and sent Captain Gore, to say it was impossible; and that, if they wanted to see a ship, they had better go to the Overyssel (a sixty-four in the Downs.) They said, no; they wanted to see me. However, I was stout, and will not be shewn about like a beast! and away they went.

I believe, Captain Gore wishes me out of his ship; for the ladies admire him, I am told, very much: but, however, no Captain could be kinder to me than he is. These ladies, he told me afterwards, were his relations.

I have just got your letters; many thanks, for them! You do not say, in the end, Sir William is arrived.

I am glad, that you approve. You may rely, my dear friend, that I will not run any unnecessary risk! No more boat work, I promise you; but, ever, your attached and faithful

NELSON & BRONTE.

To the Duke, and Lord William, say every thing which is kind; and to
 Mrs. Nelson.

I am so dreadfully sea-sick, that I cannot hold up my head!

LETTER XVII.

September 21st, [1801.]
Quarter past Ten o'Clock.

MY DEAR EMMA,

I wish you would send the letter to Mrs. Dod's, directly; for, otherwise, he may, inadvertently.

If done, and it comes to London, deliver some of the things. The wardrobe is her's; and if any of her clothes are at Mr. Dod's, they had better be separated from mine—and, indeed, what things are worth removing—to have them directly sent to Merton. A bed, or two, I believe, belong to my father; but, am not sure.

I send you Dr. Baird's comfortable note, this moment received.

You will [find] Parker is treated like an infant. Poor fellow! I trust, he will get well, and take possession of his room at the farm.

Ever your affectionate,

NELSON & BRONTE.

LETTER XVIII.

Amazon, September 26, 1801.
Eight o'Clock.

MY DEAREST EMMA,

Your kind letters came on board about six o'clock.

You may rely upon one thing, that I shall like Merton; therefore, do not be uneasy on that account. I have that opinion of your taste and judgment, that I do not believe it can fail in pleasing me. We must only consider our means; and, for the rest, I am sure, you will soon make it the prettiest place in the world.

I dare say, Mr. Hazelwood acted, like all lawyers, whose only consideration was for their client: but, I am sure, you will do, for me, all the civil things towards Mrs. Greaves.

If I can afford to buy the Duck Close, and the field adjoining, it would be pleasant; but, I fear, it is not in my power: but, I shall know, when my accounts are settled, at New Year's Day.

To be sure, we shall employ the trades-people of our village, in preference to any others, in what we want for common use, and give them every encouragement to be kind and attentive to us.

From my heart, do I wish that I was with you: and it cannot be long; for, to-day, I am far from well; violent head ache, and very cold; but, it may be agitation.

Whatever, my dear Emma, you do for my little charge, I must be pleased with. Probably, she will be lodged at Merton; at least, in the spring, when she can have the benefit of our walks. It will make the poor mother happy, I am sure.

I do not write to her to-day, as this goes through the Admiralty; but, tell her all I would say. You know my unchangeable thoughts about her.

I shall have the child christened, when I come up.

Have we a nice church at Merton? We will set an example of goodness to the under-parishioners.

Would to God, I was with you at Laleham. I shall never forget our happiness at that place.

Mr. Davison will pay Mrs. Nelson fifty pounds, October 1st. I dare say, Mr. Shakespeare has some orders about it.

I had, yesterday, a letter from my father; he seems to think, that he may do something which I shall not like. I suppose, he means, going to Somerset Street.

Shall I, to an old man, enter upon the detestable subject; it may shorten his days. But, I think, I shall tell him, that I cannot go to Somerset Street, to see him. But, I shall not write till I hear your opinion.

If I once begin, you know, it will all out, about her, and her ill-treatment to her son. But, you shall decide.

Our accounts of dear Parker, I fear, preclude all hopes of his recovery.

It was my intention to have gone ashore this morning, to have called on Admiral Lutwidge: but, the wind's coming fresh from the S.W. I have declined it; for, I doubt, if I could get off again.

At ten o'clock, with your letters, came off Dr. Baird's note, to say every hope was gone! I have desired, that his death should be sent, by telegraph, to the Admiralty. They will, surely, honour his memory, although they would not promote him.

What are our feelings, my dear Emma! but, we must cheer up: and, with best regards to Mrs. Nelson, believe me ever, for ever, your most affectionate,

NELSON & BRONTE.

Best regards to Sir William.

I send you the last report. Who knows!

LETTER XIX.

Amazon, October 8, 1801.

MY DEAREST FRIEND,

I do not expect, although I am writing, that any boat can communicate with us to-day.

What can be the use of keeping me here? for, I can know nothing such weather; and, what a change since yesterday! It came on, in one hour, from the water like a mill-head, to such a sea as to make me very unwell. If I had gone to make my visit, I could not have got off again. I rejoice that I did not go.

Until I leave the station, I have no desire to go on shore; for, Deal was always my abhorrence.

That Parker is a swindler. Langford owed our dear Parker twenty-five pounds, of which there was no account; but Langford desired his agents to pay Mr. Parker. Langford requested, that he would wait two or three months, as it would be more convenient to him. To which the other agreed—"Aye, as long as you please." He got one pound eleven shillings and sixpence from Samuel, by casting his account wrong. The first thing he does, is to desire Langford's agents to pay thirty-four pounds for Langford, nine pounds more than the debt. He is worse than a public thief. His conduct to me was, absolutely, the worst species of thieving; for, it was under false pretences. He sent Dr. Baird on board, to me, to say that, in London, his pocket book was stole, in which was twenty pounds; and begged my assistance to get him home; and that he had not a farthing to buy mourning for his dear son. At this time, he had forty-seven pounds in his pocket, besides what he had sold of his son's. He has behaved so unlike a gentleman, but very like a blackguard, to both Captain Sutton, Bedford, and Hardy, I am now clear that he never lost one farthing, and that the whole is a swindling trick. So, you see, my dear friend, how good-nature is imposed upon. I am so vexed, that he should have belonged to our dear Parker!

I have now done with the wretch, for ever. I hope he has got nothing from you; and, if you have promised him any thing, do not send it.

Ten o'Clock.

Your kind letters are arrived. I rejoice that you have got into
 Merton. I hope to get the letter on shore; but, it is very uncertain.

Ministry, my dearest friend, think very differently of my services from you! But, never mind; I shall soon have done with them afloat.

Make my kindest regards to Sir William, and all our friends; and believe me, ever, your faithful and affectionate

NELSON & BRONTE.

I have just got a very kind letter from Captain Read. He says, he will come and see me, be where it will. He inquired after you and Sir William.

LETTER XX.

Amazon, Ten o'Clock,
October 12, 1801.

MY DEAREST FRIEND,

This being a very fine morning, and smooth beach, at eight o'clock, I went with Sutton and Bedford, and landed at Walmer; but found Billy fast asleep: so, left my card; walked the same road that we came, when the carriage could not come with us that night; and all rushed into my mind, and brought tears into my eyes. Ah! how different to walking with such a friend as you, Sir William, and Mrs. Nelson.

Called at the barracks, on Lord George; but, he is gone to London.

From thence to the Admiral's, found him up; and, waiting half an hour to see Mrs. Lutwidge, who entreated me to stay dinner, came directly on board.

I did not even call to see poor Langford; who has been worse these few days past, and God knows when he will be well. I am afraid it will be a long time; for several pieces of bone are lately come away, and more to come.

But Troubridge has so completely prevented my ever mentioning any body's service, that I am become a cypher, and he has gained a victory over Nelson's spirit. I am kept here; for what, he may be able to tell, I cannot: but long it cannot, shall not, be.

Sutton and Bedford are gone a tour, till dinner time: but nothing shall make me, but almost force, go out of the ship again, till I have done; and the Admiralty, in charity, will be pleased to release me.

I am, in truth, not over well. I have a complaint in my stomach and bowels, but it will go off. If you was here, I should have some rhubarb; but, as you are not, I shall go without.

Sutton has sent into Yorkshire, for a cow that, in the spring, will give fourteen pounds of butter a week; and, he has given Allen the finest goat I ever saw. The latter, I am afraid, will be troublesome.

Just as I was coming off, I received your packet; and thank you, from my heart, for all your kindness.

What can Reverend Sir want to be made a Doctor for? He will be laughed at, for his pains!

I thank you for the King's letters, I shall write a kind line to Castelcicala, and answer the King's, very soon: and, write to Acton; for he can make Bronte every thing to me, if he pleases. I dare say, I did wrong, never to write him; but, as he treated Sir William unkindly, I never could bring myself to it.

I am glad the Duke has been to see you; and taking plants from him, is nothing. Make my kindest remembrances to him.

I would have every body like your choice; for, I am sure, you have as fine a taste in laying out land, as you have in music. I'll be damned, if Mrs. Billington can sing so well as you. She may have stage trick, but you have pure nature.

I always say every thing, for you and Sir William. I wish you had translated the King's and Acton's letters, Banti cannot.

I may be able to dispose of Charles, but not of the other, and he would corrupt Charles.

For ever yours,

NELSON & BRONTE.

Mrs. Lutwidge inquires always particularly after you. We all laugh, and say she is more fond of soldiers than ever, since General Don has shewn her how he would keep off the French!

LETTER XXI.

Amazon, October 15th, 1801.

MY DEAREST FRIEND,

I have received all your letters of yesterday, and the one sent from the post at Merton; and, also, one mis-sent to Poole: but I do not write direct to Merton, till I hear that mine to Sir William, sent yesterday, gets to you before those by London.

The Admiralty will not give me leave, till the 22d; and, then, only ten days. What a set of beasts!

My cold is now got into my head; and I have such dreadful pain in my teeth, that I cannot hold up my head: but none of them cares a damn for me or my sufferings; therefore, you see, I cannot discharge my steward.

And yet, I think, upon consideration, that I will send up all my things, and take my chance as to their sending me down again. What do you think? At all events, every thing except my bed. I have table-spoons, forks, every thing; at least, I shall have, soon, two hundred pounds worth.

What a b—— that Miss Knight is! As to the other, I care not what she says.

My poor dear father is wrong. But more of this, when we meet: which will be Friday, the 23d, at farthest; if possible, the 22d. But, the Admiralty are hard upon me.

I am sorry to hear, that you have been ill: and my cold is so dreadfully bad, that I cannot hold up my head; and am so damned stupid that you must, my dear friend, forgive my letter.

Admiral Lutwidge is going to Portsmouth. Sir William Parker is going to be tried, for something.

Make my kindest respects to Sir William; and believe me, ever, your's most faithfully,

 NELSON & BRONTE.

I have wrote a line to Merton.

Excuse my letter.

LETTER XXII.

Amazon October 16th, 1801.

MY DEAREST FRIEND,

It being a very fine morning, and the beach smooth, I went to call on
Admiral Lutwidge, and returned on board before ten o'clock.

Mrs. Lutwidge is delighted with your present. Sutton, &c. were called forth to admire it. She joins in abusing the Admiralty. She pressed me very much to dine with them at three o'clock; but, I told her I would not dine with the angel Gabriel, to be dragged through a night surf!

Her answer was, that she hoped soon I should dine with an angel, for she was sure you was one. In short, she adores you; but, who does not? You are so good, so kind, to every body; old, young, rich, or poor, it is the same thing!

I called on poor Langford; who has a long time to look forward to, for getting well; he told me your goodness, in writing him a line: and I called upon Dr. Baird; he disapproves of rhubarb, and has prescribed magnesia and peppermint: and I called on Mr. Lawrence. So, you see, I did much business in one hour I was on shore.

Civility to Lutwidge was proper for me; and, indeed, my duty.

The moment I got your letters, off I came, and have read them with real pleasure. They have made me much better, I think; at least, I feel so.

I admire the pigs and poultry. Sheep are certainly most beneficial to eat off the grass. Do you get paid for them; and take care that they are kept on the premises all night, for that is the time they do good to the land. They should be folded. Is your head man a good person, and true to our interest? I intend to have a farming book. I am glad to hear you get fish; not very good ones, I fancy.

It is, I thank God, only six days before I shall be with you, and to be shewn all the beauties of Merton. I shall like it, leaves or no leaves.

No person there can take amiss our not visiting. The answer from me will always be very civil thanks, but that I wish to live retired. We shall have our sea friends; and, I know, Sir William thinks they are the best.

I have a letter from Mr. Trevor, begging me to recommend a youngster for him; but, none before your Charles.

Banti, I suppose, must return; but, at present, we know not what ships are to be kept in commission.

I have a letter from a female relation of mine. She has had three husbands; and he, Mr. Sherstone, three wives. Her brother, a Nelson, I have been trying, ever since I have been in England, to get promoted. The last and present Admiralty promised. I never saw the man; he is in a ship in the North Seas, forty-five years of age.

I have a letter from Troubridge, recommending me to wear flannel shirts. Does he care for me? No; but, never mind. They shall work hard, to get me back again.

Remember me, kindly, to Sir William, the Duke, and all friends; and believe me, ever, your most affectionate

NELSON & BRONTE.

Do you ever see Castelcicala? He is a good man, and faithful to his master and mistress.

LETTER XXIII.

Amazon, October 16th, 1801.

MY DEAREST FRIEND,

I send you a letter for Allen's wife; and one for Germany, which I wish you would make Oliver put in the Foreign Post Office, and pay what is necessary.

I would send you the letter to which it is an answer, but it would be over-weight. It is all compliments; and, the man says, it is all truth.

The wind is freshened cold, but very fine day.

Best regards to Sir William, Mrs. Cadogan, Mr. Oliver, and all friends.

For ever, your's faithfully,

NELSON & BRONTE.

I have a letter from Reverend Doctor—he is as big as if he was a Bishop; and one from the Bedel of the university, to say how well he preached. I hope you ordered something good for him, for those big wigs love eating and drinking.

LETTER XXIV.

Amazon, October 17th, 1801.

MY DEAREST FRIEND,

Although my complaint has no danger attending it, yet it resists the medicines which Dr. Baird has prescribed; and, I fancy, it has pulled me down very much.

The cold has settled in my bowels. I wish the Admiralty had my complaint: but, they have no bowels; at least, for me.

I had a very indifferent night, but your and Sir William's kind letters have made me feel better.

I send you a letter from Lord Pelham. I shall certainly attend; and let them see, that I may be useful in council as I have been in the field. We must submit; and, perhaps, these Admiralty do this by me, to prevent another application.

You may rely, that I shall be with you by dinner, on Friday; at half past three, or four at farthest.

I shall not dine with Pitt, as Mr. and Mrs. Long are staying there.
Not that I ever saw her in my life, nor care if I never do.

I pray that I may not be annoyed, on my arrival: it is retirement with my friends, that I wish for.

Thank Sir William, kindly, for his letter; and the inclosure, which I return.

Sutton is much pleased with your letter; and, with Bedford, will certainly make you a visit. They are both truly good and kind to me.

Our weather has been cold these two days, but not bad. I have got a fire in the cabin; and, I hope my complaint will go off.

May Heaven bless you!

I send this, through Troubridge, direct in Piccadilly.

I shall, you may rely, admire the pig-stye, ducks, fowls, &c. for every thing you do, I look upon as perfect.

Dr. Baird has been aboard, to see me. He thinks, I shall be better; and, that a few days on shore will set me up again.

Make my kind remembrances to Sir William, the Duke, and all friends; and believe me, ever, your most affectionate

NELSON & BRONTE.

Bedford has made me laugh. Mrs. Lutwidge has been babbling, that she will go to Portsmouth with the Admiral; who says, he shall be so fully employed that he cannot be much with her. She whispered Bedford—"I have many friends in the army there!"

She will certainly marry a soldier, if ever she is disposable. But, perhaps, you will agree with me, that no good soldier would take her. I am sure, the purchase would be dear, even if it was a gift. Don't call this a bull.

Sutton's man was on the farm; and the sheep, when not belonging to the farm, always paid so much sheep, so much lambs: but, I dare say, you manage well.

Sir William's letter has delighted me, with your activity and prudence.

LETTER XXV.

The two letters would have been over-weight, so I send you the letter
 I have answered. Pray, take care of it, it is a curiosity!

Ever your faithful

 NELSON & BRONTE.

 Amazon, 2 P.M.

Yawkins is in great distress: his cutter paid off; and he, like many others, very little to live upon. He begs his best respects to Sir William. He breakfasted here this morning.

Many very long faces at peace!

LETTER XXVI.

MY DEAREST FRIEND,

Hardy begs you will send the inclosed to Naples.

I wish Tyson would come home; for many are pulling at him, and I want to pay him. I will not be in his debt forty-eight hours after his arrival.

Hardy is just anchored, and his commodore gone on shore.

Ever your most faithful

NELSON & BRONTE.

Mrs. Nelson had better direct her letters to me, unless I am on the spot. You see, you paid postage, and it lays me open to their Post Office conversation.

LETTER XXVII.

Amazon, October 19th, 1801.

MY DEAREST FRIEND,

What a gale we have had! But Admiral Lutwidge's boat came off; and, as your letter was wrote, it got on shore: at least, I hope so; for the boat seemed absolutely swallowed up in the sea. None of our boats could have kept above water a moment; therefore, I could not answer all the truly friendly things you told me in your letters, for they were not opened before the boat was gone.

I am sure, you did well to send Mrs. Lutwidge a gown, and she loves you very much, but there is no accounting for taste. She admires entirely red coats; you, true blue.

They dine with Billy Pitt, to-day; or, rather, with Mr. Long; for Pitt does not keep house, in appearance, although he asked me to come and see him: and that I shall do, out of respect to a great man, although he never did any thing for me or my relations. I assure you, my dear friend, that I had rather read and hear all your little story of a white hen getting into a tree, an anecdote of Fatima, or hear you call—"Cupidy! Cupidy!" than any speech I shall hear in parliament: because I know, although you can adapt your language and manners to a child, yet that you can also thunder forth such a torrent of eloquence, that corruption and infamy would sink before your voice, in however exalted a situation it might be placed.

Poor Oliver! what can be the matter with him?

I must leave my cot here, till my discharge, when it shall come to the farm, as cots are the best things in the world for our sea friends.

Why not have the pictures from Davison's, and those from Dodd's; especially, my father's, and Davison's?

A-propos! Sir William has not sat, I fear, to Beechey. I want a half-length, the size of my father's and Davison's.

I wonder your pictures are not come from Hamburg! You have not lost the directions for unfolding them; nor the measure, that I may have frames made for them? For, up they shall go, as soon as they arrive. What, have your picture, and not hang it up? No; I will submit, in the farm, to every order but that.

The weather, to-day, is tolerable; but, I do not think I could well get on shore: but Thursday, I hope, will be a fine day.

I shall call on Mr. Pitt, make my visit at the Hospital, and get off very early on Friday morning.

My cold is still very troublesome, I cannot get my bowels in order. In the night I had not a little fever.

But, never mind; the Admiralty will not always be there. Every one has their day.

God bless you, my dear friend; and believe me, ever, your's most faithfully,

NELSON & BRONTE.

Write on Wednesday.

Your letters of yesterday are received. Reverend Doctor would like to be a Bishop.

I have sent poor Thomson's letter, and the distressed Mrs. ———, to the Earl. Kindest regards to Sir William.

LETTER XXVIII.

Amazon, October 20th, 1801.

MY DEAREST FRIEND,

How could you think, for a moment, that I would be a time-server to any Minister on earth! And, if you had studied my letter a little closer, you would have seen that my intention was, to shew them that I could be as useful in the cabinet as in the field.

My idea is, to let them see that my attendance is worth soliciting. For myself, I can have nothing; but, for my brother, something may be done.

Living with Mr. Addington a good deal; never, in your sense of the word, shall I do it. What, leave my dearest friends, to dine with a minister? Damn me, if I do, beyond what you yourself shall judge to be necessary! Perhaps, it may be once; and once with the Earl but that you shall judge for me.

If I give up all intercourse—you know enough of Courts, that they will do nothing: make yourself of consequence to them, and they will do what you wish, in reason; and, out of reason, I never should ask them.

It must be a great bore, to me, to go to the House. I shall tell Mr. Addington, that I go on the 29th to please him, and not to please myself; but more of this subject, when we meet.

Dr. Baird is laid up with the rheumatism; he will now believe, that the cold may affect me. This is the coldest place in England, most assuredly.

Troubridge writes me that, as the weather is set in fine again, he hopes I shall get walks on shore. He is, I suppose, laughing at me; but, never mind.

I agree with you, in wishing Sir William had a horse. Why don't you send to the Duke, for a poney for him.

I am just parting with four of my ships—Captains Conn, Rowley, Martin, and Whitter—who are proceeding to the Nore, in their way to be paid off.

The surf is still so great on the beach, that I could not land dry, if it was necessary, to-day; but, I hope, it will be smooth on Thursday: if not, I must go in a boat to Dover, and come from thence to Deal.

Sutton says, he will get the Amazon under sail, and carry me down; for, that I shall not take cold: Bedford goes with a squadron to Margate; so that all our party will be broke up. I am sure, to many of them, I feel truly obliged.

Make my kindest respects to Sir William; and believe me, ever, your most faithful and affectionate

NELSON & BRONTE.

I wish Banti was separated from Charles, for he is a knowing one. I wish I could get him with a good Captain, who would keep him strict to his duty.

Hardy cannot get paid a hundred pounds he advanced for Mr. Williams's nephew.

Many thanks for Mrs. Nelson's letters.

The Reverend Doctor likes going about. Only think of his wanting to come up with an address of thanks! Why, [the] King will not receive him, although he is a Doctor; and less, for being my brother—for, they certainly do not like me.

LETTER XXIX.

Amazon, October 20th, 1801.

MY DEAREST FRIEND,

Only two days more, the Admiralty could, with any conscience, keep me here; not that I think, they have had any conscience.

I dare say, Master Troubridge is grown fat. I know, I am grown lean, with my complaint: which, but for their indifference about my health, would never have happened; or, at least, I should have got well, long ago, in a warm room, with a good fire, and sincere friends.

I believe, I leave this little squadron with sincere regret, and with the good wishes of every creature in it.

How I should laugh, to see you, my dear friend, rowing in a boat; the beautiful Emma rowing a one-armed Admiral in a boat! It will certainly be caricatured.

Well done, farmer's wife! I'll bet your turkey against Mrs. Nelson's; but, Sir William and I will decide.

Hardy says, you may be sure of him; and, that he has not lost his appetite.

You will make us rich, with your economy.

I did not think, tell Sir William, that impudence had got such deep root in Wales. I send you the letter, as a curiosity; and to have the impudence to recommend a midshipman!

It is not long ago, a person from Yorkshire desired me to lend him three hundred pounds, as he was going to set up a school!

Are these people mad; or, do they take me for quite a fool?

However, I have wisdom enough to laugh at their folly; and to be, myself, your most obliged and faithful friend,

NELSON & BRONTE.

Best regards to Sir William, Mrs. Cadogan, and all friends.

LETTER XXX.

Amazon, October 21st, 1801.

MY DEAREST FRIEND,

It blows strong from the westward, and is a very dirty day, with a good deal of surf on the beach; but Hardy and Sutton recommended my going on shore this morning, as they believe it may blow a heavy gale to-morrow. But, what comfort could I have had, for two whole days, at Deal?

I hope the morning will be fine: but I have ordered a Deal boat, as they understand the beach better than our's; and, if I cannot land here, I shall go to Ramsgate Pier, and come to Deal in a carriage.

Has Mrs. Cadogan got my Peer's robe? for I must send for Mr. Webb, and have it altered to a Viscount's.

Lord Hood wrote to me, to-day, and he is to be one of my introducers. He wanted me to dine with him the 24th; but I'll be damned if I dine from home that day, and it would be as likely we should dine out the 23d.

If you and Sir William ever wish me to dine with his brother, it must be the time of a very small party; for it would be worse than death to me, to dine in so large a party.

I expect, that all animals will increase where you are, for I never expect that you will suffer any to be killed.

I am glad Sir William has got the Duke's poney; riding will do him much good.

I am sorry to tell you, that Dr. Baird is so ill, that I am told it is very probable he may never recover.

This place is the devil's, for dreadful colds: and I don't believe I should get well all the winter; for both cough, and bowels, are still very much out of order.

You are now writing your last letter for Deal; so am I, for Merton, from Deal: at least, I hope so; for, if I can help it, I will not return to it.

I have much to do, being the last day on board; but ever, my dearest friend, believe me your truly affectionate

NELSON & BRONTE.

I am literally starving with cold; but my heart is warm.

I suppose I shall dine with Lutwidge: but I am not very desirous of it; for I shall have Sutton, Bedford, and Hardy, with me.

You must prepare Banti's mother, as it is a peace, for some other line of life than the navy. Yesterday, he sold a pair of silver buckles; he would soon ruin poor Charles, who is really a well-disposed boy.

I never shall get warm again, I believe. I cannot feel the pen.

Make my kindest regards to Sir William, Mrs. Cadogan, Oliver, &c.
 Sutton, Hardy, and Bedford, all join in kind remembrances.

As Monday is Horace's birth-day, I suppose I must send him a one pound note.

LETTER XXXI.

May 22d, [1803.]
Eight o'Clock in the Morning.

MY DEAREST EMMA,

We are now in sight of Ushant, and shall see Admiral Cornwallis in an hour.

I am not in a little fret, on the idea that he may keep the Victory, and turn us all into the Amphion. It will make it truly uncomfortable; but, I cannot help myself.

I assure you, my dear Emma, that I feel a thorough conviction, that we shall meet again, with honour, riches, and health, and remain together till a good old age. I look at your and my God's Child's picture; but, till I am sure of remaining here, I cannot bring myself to hang them up. Be assured, that my attachment, and affectionate regard, is unalterable; nothing can shake it! And, pray, say so to my dear Mrs. T. when you see her. Tell her, that my love is unbounded, to her and her dear sweet child; and, if she should have more, it will extend to all of them. In short, my dear Emma, say every thing to her, which your dear, affectionate, heart and head, can think of.

We are very comfortable. Mr. Elliot is happy, has quite recovered his spirits; he was very low, at Portsmouth. George Elliot is very well; say so, to Lord Minto. Murray, Sutton—in short, every body in the ship, seems happy; and, if we should fall in with a French man-of-war, I have no fears but they will do as we used to do.

Hardy is gone into Plymouth, to see our Dutchman safe. I think, she will turn out a good prize.

Gaetano desires his duty to Miledi! He is a good man; and, I dare say, will come back: for, I think, it cannot be a long war; just enough to make me independent in pecuniary matters.

If the wind stands, on Tuesday we shall be on the coast of Portugal; and, before next Sunday, in the Mediterranean.

To Mrs. Cadogan, say every kind thing; to good Mrs. Nelson, the
Doctor, &c. &c.

If you like, you may tell him about the entailing of the pension: but, perhaps, he will be so much taken up with Canterbury, that it will do for some dull evening at Hilborough.

I shall now stop, till I have been on board the Admiral. Only, tell Mrs. T. that I will write her the first safe opportunity; I am not sure of this.

I shall direct to Merton, after June 1st. Therefore, as you change, make Davison take a direction to Nepean; but, I would not trouble him with too many directions, for fear of embroil.

May 23d.

We were close in with Brest, yesterday; and found, by a frigate, that Admiral Cornwallis had a rendezvous at sea. Thither we went; but, to this hour, cannot find him.

It blows strong. What wind we are losing! If I cannot find the Admiral by six o'clock, we must all go into the Amphion, and leave the Victory, to my great mortification. So much for the wisdom of my superiors.

I keep my letter open to the last: for, I still hope; as, I am sure, there is no good reason for my not going out in the Victory.

I am just embarking in the Amphion; cannot find Admiral Cornwallis.

May God in Heaven bless you! prays your most sincere

NELSON & BRONTE.

Stephens's publication I should like to have.

I have left my silver seal; at least, I cannot find it.

LETTER XXXII.

[July 1803.

MY DEAREST EMMA,

Although I have wrote letters from various places, merely to say—"Here I am," and "There I am;"—yet, as I have no doubt but that they would all be read, it was impossible for me to say more than—"Here I am, and well:" and I see no prospect of any certain mode of conveyance, but by sea; which, with the means the Admiralty has given me, of small vessels, can be but seldom.

Our passages have been enormously long. From Gibraltar to Malta, we were eleven days: arriving the fifteenth in the evening, and sailing in the night of the sixteenth—that is, three in the morning of the seventeenth—and it was the twenty-sixth before we got off Capri; where I had ordered the frigate, which carried Mr. Elliot to Naples, to join me.

I send you copies of the King and Queen's letters. I am vexed, that she did not mention you! I can only account for it, by her's being a political letter.

When I wrote to the Queen, I said—"I left Lady Hamilton, the eighteenth of May; and so attached to your Majesty, that I am sure she would lay down her life to preserve your's. Your Majesty never had a more sincere, attached, and real friend, than your dear Emma. You will be sorry to hear, that good Sir William did not leave her in such comfortable circumstances as his fortune would have allowed. He has given it amongst his relations. But she will do honour to his memory, although every one else of his friends call loudly against him on that account."

I trust, my dear Emma, she has wrote you. If she can forget Emma, I hope, God will forget her! But, you think, that she never will, or can. Now is her time to shew it.

You will only shew the King and Queen's letters to some few particular friends.

The King is very low; lives, mostly, at Belvidere. Mr. Elliot had not seen either him or the Queen, from the seventeenth, the day of his arrival, to the twenty-first. On the next day, he was to be presented.

I have made up my mind, that it is part of the plan of that Corsican Scoundrel, to conquer the kingdom of Naples. He has marched thirteen thousand men into the kingdom, on the Adriatic side; and he will take possession, with as much shadow of right, of Gaeta and Naples: and, if the poor King remonstrates, or allows us to secure Sicily, he will call it war, and declare a conquest.

I have cautioned General Acton, not to risk the Royal Family too long; but Naples will be conquered, sooner or later, as it may suit Buonaparte's convenience.

The Morea, and Egypt, are likewise in his eye. An army of full seventy thousand men are assembling in Italy.

Gibbs and Noble are gone to Malta.

I am, you may believe, very anxious to get off Toulon, to join the fleet.

Sir Richard Bickerton went from off Naples, the day I left Gibraltar.

We passed Monte Christo, Bastia, and Cape Corse, yesterday; and are now moving, slowly, direct for Toulon.

What force they have, I know not; indeed, I am totally ignorant: some say, nine sail of the line; some, seven; some, five. If the former, they will come out; for we have only the same number, including sixty-fours, and very shortly manned.

However, I hope they will come out, and let us settle the matter. You know, I hate being kept in suspence.

[July 8th.

I left this hole, to put down what force the French have at Toulon. Seven sail of the line ready, five frigates, and six corvettes. One or two more in about a week. We, to day, eight sail of the line—to-morrow, seven; including two sixty-four gun ships.

You will readily believe, how rejoiced I shall be to get one of your dear, excellent letters, that I may know every thing which has passed since my absence.

I sincerely hope, that Mr. Booth has settled all your accounts. Never mind, my dear Emma, a few hundred pounds; which is all the rigid gripe of the law, not justice, can wrest from you.

I thank God, that you cannot want; (although that is no good reason for its being taken from you:) whilst I have sixpence, you shall not want for fivepence of it! But, you have bought your experience, that there is no friendship in money concerns; and, your good sense will make you profit of it.

I hope, the minister has done something for you. But, never mind, we can live upon bread and cheese.

Independence is a blessing; and, although I have not yet found out the way to get prize money—what has been taken, has run into our mouths—however, it must turn out very hard, if I cannot get enough to pay off my debts, and that will be no small comfort.

I have not mentioned my Bronte affairs to Acton, as yet; but, if Naples remains much longer, I shall ask the question. But, I expect nothing from them. I believe, even Acton wishes himself well, and safely removed.

I think, from what I hear, that the King's spirits are so much depressed, that he will give up the reins of Naples, at least, to his son, and retire to Sicily. Sir William, you know, always thought, that he would end his life so. Certainly, his situation must be heart-breaking!

Gaetano returned in the frigate. I believe, he saw enough of Naples. He carried his family money; and Mr. Falconet (Gibbs being absent) will pay Mr. Greville's pension to Gaetano's family. I have now [sent] Gaetano to the post: and he desires, to present his duty; and to tell you, that Mr. Ragland, from Sir William's death, will not pay any more pensions, without orders from Mr. Greville.

Vincenzo has had none paid. He is very poor; keeps a shop. His son wanted, I find, to come in the frigate to me. I cannot afford to maintain him; therefore, I shall give no encouragement.

Old Antonio was allowed a carline a day; that is, now, not paid.

Sabatello lives with Mr. Elliot.

Nicolo, and Mary Antonio, have left Mr. Gibbs, for some cause; Gaetano says, he believes, for amore.

Francesca has two children living, and another coming. She lives the best amongst them, like gallant homme.

Pasqual lives with the Duke Montelione; and Joseph, with the old
 Russian.

Your house is a hotel; the upper parts are kept for the Marquis, the owner.

Mr. Elliot has taken the house of the Baille Franconi, on the Chaia.

Doctor Nudi inquired kindly after us; and all the women at Santa Lucia expected, when they saw Gaetano, that you was arrived.

Bread never was so dear; every thing else in plenty. The wages not being raised, Gaetano says, the poor of England are a million times better off.

So much for Gaetano's news. He desires his duty to Signora Madre; and remembrances to Mary Ann, Fatima, &c.

[July 8th.

We joined, this morning, the fleet. The men in the ships are good; but the ships themselves are a little the worse for wear, and very short of their complements of men. We shall never be better: therefore, let them come; the sooner, the better.

I shall write a line to the Duke, that he may see I do not forget my friends; and I rely, my dearest Emma, on your saying every kind thing, for me, to the Doctor, Mrs. Nelson, Mrs. Bolton, Mr. and Mrs. Matcham, Mrs. Cadogan; whose kindness, and goodness, I shall never forget.

You will have the goodness to send the inclosed, as directed; and be assured, that I am, to the last moment of my life, your most attached, faithful, and affectionate,

NELSON & BRONTE.

LETTER XXXIII.

Victory, off Toulon,
August 1, 1803.

[I do not know that you will get this letter.]

MY DEAREST EMMA,

Your letter of May 31, which came under cover to Mr. Noble, of Naples, inclosing Davison's correspondence with Plymouth, arrived by the Phoebe two days ago: and this is the only scrap of a pen which has been received by any person in the fleet since we sailed from England.

You will readily conceive, my dear Emma, the sensations which the sight and reading even your few lines [occasioned.] They cannot be understood, but by those of such mutual and truly sincere attachment as your's and mine. Although you said little, I understood a great deal, and most heartily approve of your plan and society for next winter; and, next spring, I hope to be rich enough to begin the alterations at dear Merton. It will serve to amuse you; and, I am sure, that I shall admire all your alterations, even to planting a gooseberry bush.

Sutton joined me yesterday, and we are all got into the Victory; and, a few days will put us in order.

Every body gives a very excellent character of Mr. Chevalier, the servant recommended by Mr. Davison; and I shall certainly live as frugal as my station will admit. I have known the pinch, and shall endeavour never to know it again.

I want to send two thousand one hundred pounds, to pay off Mrs. Greaves, on October 1st. But, I have not received one farthing; but, I hope to receive some soon. But Mr. Haslewood promised to see this matter kept right for me.

Hardy is now busy, hanging up your and Horatia's picture; and I trust soon to see the other two safe arrived from the Exhibition. I want no others to ornament my cabin. I can contemplate them, and find new beauties every day, and I do not want any body else.

You will not expect much news from us. We see nothing. I have great fear, that all Naples will fall into the hands of the French; and, if Acton does not take care, Sicily also. However, I have given my final advice so fully and strongly that, let what will happen, they cannot blame me.

Captain Capel says, Mr. Elliot cannot bear Naples. I have no doubt, but that it is very different to your time.

The Queen, I fancy, by the seal, has sent a letter to Castelcicala; her letter to me is only thanks for my attention to the safety of the kingdom. If Dr. Scott has time, and is able, he shall write a copy for you.

The King is very much retired. He would not see the French General, St. Cyr; who came to Naples, to settle the contribution for the payment of the French army.

The Queen was ordered to give him and the French minister a dinner, but the King staid at Belvidere.

I think, he will give it up soon; and retire to Sicily, if the French will allow him.

Acton has never dared give Mr. Elliot, or one Englishman, a dinner.

The fleet are ready to come forth; but, they will not come for the sake of fighting me.

I have this day made George Elliot, post; Lieutenant Pettit, a master and commander; and Mr. Hindmarsh, gunner's son, of the Bellerophon, who behaved so well this day five year, a Lieutenant.

I reckon to have lost two French seventy-fours, by my not coming out in the Victory; but I hope they will come soon, with interest.

This goes to Gibraltar, by Sutton, in the Amphion.

I shall write the Doctor in a day or two. I see, by the French papers, that he has kissed hands.

With kindest regards to your good mother, and all at Merton, &c. &c. &c. ever your's, most faithfully and affectionately,

  NELSON & BRONTE.

LETTER XXXIV.

Victory, off Toulon,
August 10th, 1803.

MY DEAREST EMMA,

I take the opportunity of Mr. Acourt's going through Spain, with Mr. Elliot's dispatches for England, to send this letter: for I would not, for the world, miss any opportunity of sending you a line.

By Gibraltar, I wrote you, as lately as the 4th; but all our ways of communicating with England, are very uncertain: and, I believe, the Admiralty must have forgot us; for, not a vessel of any kind or sort has joined us, since I left Spithead.

News, I absolutely am ignorant of: except, that a schooner, belonging to me, put her nose into Toulon; and four frigates popped out, and have taken her, and a transport loaded with water for the fleet. However, I hope to have an opportunity, very soon, of paying them the debt, with interest.

Mr. Acourt says, at Naples, they hope that the mediation of Russia will save them: but, I doubt, if Russia will go to war with the French for any kingdom; and they, poor souls! relying on a broken reed, will lose Sicily.

As for getting any thing for Bronte, I cannot expect it; for, the finances of Naples are worse than ever. Patienza, however; I will— *

I see, many Bishops are dead. Is my brother tired of Canterbury? I wish I could make him a Bishop. If you see him, or write, say that I have not ten minutes to send away Mr. Acourt, who cannot be detained.

I hope Lord St. Vincent has sent out Sir William Bolton. As soon as I know who is first Lord, I will write him.

LETTER XXXV.

MY DEAR LADY HAMILTON,

Your friend's godson arrived safe yesterday afternoon; and I shall, you know, always feel too happy in obeying your commands: for, you never ask favours, but for your friends.

In short, in every point of view, from Ambassatrice to the duties of domestic life, I never saw your equal!

That elegance of manners; accomplishments; and, above all, your goodness of heart, is unparalleled: and only believe, for ever, and beyond it, your faithful and devoted

 NELSON & BRONTE.

Victory, August 24th, 1803.

LETTER XXXVI.

[N.B. The Mysterious Letter appears to have been inclosed in this Packet.]

August 26th, 1803.
Wrote several days past.

MY DEAREST EMMA,

By the Canopus, Admiral Campbell, I have received all your truly kind and affectionate letters, from May 20th to July 3d; with the exception of one, dated May 31st, sent to Naples.

This is the first communication I have had with England since we sailed.

All your letters, my dear letters, are so entertaining! and which paint so clearly what you are after, that they give me either the greatest pleasure or pain. It is the next best thing, to being with you.

I only desire, my dearest Emma, that you will always believe, that Nelson's your own; Nelson's Alpha and Omega is Emma! I cannot alter; my affection and love is beyond even this world! Nothing can shake it, but yourself; and that, I will not allow myself to think, for a moment, is possible.

I feel, that you are the real friend of my bosom, and dearer to me than life; and, that I am the same to you. But, I will neither have P.'s nor Q.'s come near you! No; not the slice of Single Gloster! But, if I was to go on, it would argue that want of confidence which would be injurious to your honour.

I rejoice that you have had so pleasant a trip into Norfolk; and I hope, one day, to carry you there by a nearer tie in law, but not in love and affection, than at present.

I wish, you would never mention that person's name! It works up your anger, for no useful purpose. Her good or bad character, of me or thee, no one cares about.

This letter will find you at dear Merton; where we shall one day meet, and be truly happy.

I do not think it can be a long war; and, I believe, it will be much shorter than people expect: and I shall hope to find the new room built; the grounds laid out, neatly but not expensively; new Piccadilly gates; kitchen garden; &c. Only let us have a plan, and then all will go on well. It will be a great source of amusement to you; and Horatia shall plant a tree. I dare say, she will be very busy. Mrs. Nelson, or Mrs. Bolton, &c. will be with you; and time will pass away, till I have the inexpressible happiness of arriving at Merton. Even the thought of it vibrates through my nerves; for, my love for you is as unbounded as the ocean!

I feel all your good mother's kindness; and, I trust, that we shall turn rich, by being economists. Spending money, to please a pack of people, is folly, and without thanks. I desire, that you will say every kind thing from me to her, and make her a present of something in my name.

Dr. Scott is gone with my mission to Algiers, or I would send you a copy of the King and Queen's letter. I send you one from the Queen. Both King, Queen, and Acton, were very civil to Sir William Bolton. He dined with Acton.

Bolton does very well in his brig; but, he has made not a farthing of prize money. If I knew where to send him for some, he should go; but, unless we have a Spanish war, I shall live here at a great expence: although Mr. Chevalier takes every care, and I have great reason to be satisfied.

I have just asked William, who behaves very well, whether he chooses to remit any of his wages to his father. It does not appear, he does, at present. He is paid, by the King, eighteen pounds a year, as one of my retinue; therefore I have nothing to pay. I have told him, whenever he chooses to send any, to tell Mr. Scott, or Captain Hardy, and he will receive a remittance bill; so, he may now act as he pleases.

A-propos of Mr. Scott. He is very much obliged to you for your news of Mrs. Scott's being brought to bed. No letters came in the cutter, but to me, and he was very uneasy. He is a very excellent good man; and, I am very fortunate in having such a one.

I admire your kindness to my dear sister Bolton. I have wrote her, that certainly I will assist Tom Bolton at college. It is better, as I tell her, not to promise more than I am sure I can perform. It is only doing them a injury. I tell her, if vacancies, please God, should happen, that my income will be much increased.

With respect to Mr. Bolton—every body knows, that I have no interest; nobody cares for me: but, if he will point out what he wants, I will try what can be done. But, I am sure, he will not be half so well off as at present. Supposing he could get a place of a few hundreds a year, he would be a ten times poorer man than he is at present. I could convince you of it, in a moment; but, if I was to begin, then it would be said, I wanted inclination to render them a service.

I should like to see Sir H―― P――'s book. I cannot conceive how a man that is reported to have been so extravagant of government's money, to say no worse, can make a good story.

I wrote to the old Duke, not long since. I regard him; but, I would not let him touch you for all his money. No; that would never do!

I believe Mr. Bennett's bill to be correct; but, it was not intended you should pay that out of the allowance for Merton; and, how could you afford to send Mrs. Bolton a hundred pounds. It is impossible, out of your income.

I wish Mr. Addington would give you five hundred pounds a year; then, you would be better able to give away than at present. But your purse, my dear Emma, will always be empty; your heart is generous beyond your means.

Your good mother is always sure of my sincerest regard; pray, tell her so.

Connor is getting on very well: but, I cannot ask Captain Capel to rate him; that must depend upon the boy's fitness, and Capel's kindness. I have placed another year's allowance of thirty pounds in Capel's hands, and given Connor a present.

What a story, about Oliver and Mr. Matcham buying an estate in Holstein; and, to sell out at such a loss! I never heard the like. I sincerely hope it will answer his expectations; it is a fine country, but miserably cold.

How can Tyson be such a fool! I sincerely hope, he will never want money. I am not surprised at Troubridge's abuse; but, his tongue is no scandal. You make me laugh, when you imitate the Doctor!

I am quite delighted with Miss Yonge's goodness: and I beg you will make my best respects to her and her good father; and assure Mr. Yonge, how much obliged I feel for all his kind attentions to you. Those who do that, are sure of a warm place in my esteem.

I have wrote to Dumourier; therefore, I will only trouble you to say how much I respect him. I fancy he must have suffered great distress at Altona. However, I hope, he will now be comfortable for life. He is a very clever man; and beats our Generals, out and out. Don't they feel his coming? Advise him not to make enemies, by shewing he knows more than some of us. Envy knows no bounds to its persecution. He has seen the world, and will be on his guard.

I put Suckling into a frigate, with a very good man, who has a schoolmaster; he does very well. Bulkley will be a most excellent sea-officer; it is a pity he has not served his time. I have answered Mr. Suckling's letter.

Gaetano is very well, and desires his duty. I think, sometimes, that he wishes to be left at Naples; but, I am not sure.

Mr. Denis's relation has been long in the Victory; but, if the Admiralty will not promote my lieutenants, they must all make a retrograde motion. But, I hope, they will not do such a cruel thing. I have had a very affectionate letter from Lord Minto. I hope George will be confirmed; but, the Earl will not answer his application.

I shall send you some sherry, and a cask of paxoretti, by the convoy. Perhaps, it had better go to Merton, at once; or, to Davison's cellar, where the wine-cooper can draw it off. I have two pipes of sherry, that is bad; but, if you like, you can send the Doctor a hogshead of that which is coming. Davison will pay all the duties. Send it entirely free, even to the carriage. You know, doing the thing well, is twice doing it; for, sometimes, carriage is more thought of than the prime cost.

The paxoretti I have given to Davison; and ordered one hogshead of sherry to Canterbury, and one to dear Merton.

LETTER XXXVII.

Victory, September 10th, 1803.

MY DEAREST EMMA,

What can I send you, buffeting the stormy gulph of Lyons; nothing, but my warmest affection, in return for all your goodness to me and mine!

I have sent to Naples, to try and get some shawls from the King's manufactory; and have requested Mr. Falconet to ask his wife to choose some for you, and also some fine Venetian chains. I only wish, my dear Emma, that I knew what you would like, and I would order them with real pleasure; therefore, pray tell me.

We have so very little communication with the Mediterranean world, Malta and Toulon are in separate worlds. It takes, on the [average,] six or seven weeks to get an answer to a letter: and, in fifteen to twenty days, by the French papers, which we get from Paris, we have news from London; not the best side of the question, you may be sure, but enough to give us an idea of how matters go on.

I am of opinion, that we shall have a peace much sooner than is generally expected: and that will be, to me, the very highest pleasure in this world; to return to Merton, and your dear beloved society. Then, I agree with you, that "I would not give sixpence to call the King my uncle!"

I have wrote again to Gibbs, about my Bronte affairs; and [the copy of a letter] to Mrs. Græfer I will send you, if I can; but you must preserve it, for I have no other. It may be necessary, situated as I am, to keep her in good humour; for a thousand pounds may be easily sold off the estate, and I never the wiser. However, you will see what I have said.

I have wrote to Mr. Elliot about Sabatello. What a rascal he must be! Gaetano is going to Naples, and I shall tell him; but, of course, he would rather favour Sabatello, his brother-in-law, than Julia.

I send you, my dearest Emma, an hundred pounds, which you will dispose of as follows—a present for yourself; and, if you like, a trifle to the servants: something to the poor of Merton; something for Mrs. Cadogan, Miss Connor, Charlotte, &c. &c. I only send this as a trifling remembrance from me, whose whole soul is at Merton.

September 16th.

The day after I wrote the former part of this letter, Mr. Scott received from Venice, and desired to present to you, two very handsome Venetian chains, received from Venice. This I would not suffer; for I allow no one to make my own Emma presents, but her Nelson. Therefore, he will be paid for them; but, your obligation is not the less to him. He is a very worthy, excellent, modest man, and an excellent secretary.

Dr. Scott is, at times, wrong in the head; absolutely, too much learning has turned him. But we all go on very well.

I had a letter from Gibbs about Bronte, and from Noble, which will begin another letter; only, believe me, at all times, sides, and ends, most faithfully your's, for ever,

NELSON & BRONTE.

LETTER XXXVIII.

September 26th, 1803.

MY DEAREST EMMA,

We have had, for these fourteen days past, nothing but gales of wind, and a heavy sea. However, as our ships have suffered no damage, I hope to be able to keep the sea all the winter. Nothing, but dire necessity, shall force me to that out of the way place, Malta. If I had depended upon that island, for supplies for the fleet, we must all have been knocked up, long ago; for, Sir Richard Bickerton sailed from Malta, the same day I left Portsmouth. So that we have been a pretty long cruise; and, if I had only to look to Malta for supplies, our ships companies would have been done for long ago. However, by management, I have got supplies from Spain, and also from France; but it appears, that we are almost shut out from Spain, for they begin to be very uncivil to our ships. However, I suppose, by this time, something is settled; but, I never hear from England. My last letters are July 6th, near three months. But, as I get French newspapers occasionally, we guess how matters are going on.

I have wrote Mr. Gibbs, again, a long history about Bronte; and, I hope, if General Acton will do nothing for me, that he will settle something: but, I know, whatever is settled, I shall be the loser. Till next year, the debt will not be paid off; how—

* *

LETTER XXXIX.

Victory, off Toulon,
October 18th, 1803.

MY DEAREST EMMA,

Your truly kind and affectionate letters, from July 17th, to August 24th, all arrived safe in the Childers, the 6th of this month.

Believe me, my beloved Emma, that I am truly sensible of all your love and affection, which is reciprocal. You have, from the variety of incidents passing before you, much to tell me; and, besides, you have that happy knack of making every thing you write interesting. Here I am, one day precisely like the other; except the difference of a gale of wind, or not.

Since September 1st, we have not had four fine days; and, if the French do not come out soon, I fear, some of my ships will cry out.

You are very good, to send me your letters to read.

Mrs. D—— is a damned pimping bitch! What has she to do with your love? She would have pimped for Lord B——, or Lord L——, or Captain M'N——, * * * * of * * * *, or any one else. She is all vanity: fancies herself beautiful; witty; in short, like you. She be damned!

As I wrote you, the consulship at Civita Vecchia will not, in itself, pay their lodgings; and, the bad air will tip her off.

There will be no Lord Bristol's table. He tore his last will, a few hours before his death. It is said, that it was giving every thing to those devils of Italians about him.

I wish he may have given Mrs. Denis any thing; but, I do not think it: and, as for you, my dear Emma, as long as I can, I don't want any of their gifts.

As for old Q. he may put you into his will, or scratch you out, as he pleases, I care not.

If Mr. Addington gives you the pension, it is well; but, do not let it fret you. Have you not Merton? It is clear—the first purchase—and my dear Horatia is provided for: and, I hope, one of these days, that you will be my own Duchess of Bronte; and, then, a fig for them all!

I have just had a letter from Gibbs, of which I send you a copy. You see what interest he is taking about Bronte.

I begin to think, without some assistance like his, that I never should have touched a farthing. It will be 1805, before I touch the estate. Neither principal or interest of the seven thousand ounces have been paid; and, it is now eight thousand ounces debt.

You will see, Gibbs, at last, has fixed on sending his daughter home; and I shall be glad of so good an opportunity of obliging him, as it will naturally tie him to my interest. He was a great fool, not to have sent the child with you, as you wished.

I am glad to find, my dear Emma, that you mean to take Horatia home. Aye! she is like her mother; will have her own way, or kick up a devil of a dust. But, you will cure her: I am afraid I should spoil her; for, I am sure, I would shoot any one who would hurt her.

She was always fond of my watch; and, very probably, I might have promised her one: indeed, I gave her one, which cost sixpence! But, I go no where to get any thing pretty; therefore, do not think me neglectful.

I send you Noble's letter; therefore, I hope you will get your cases in good order: they have had some narrow escapes.

I am glad you liked South End.

How that Coffin could come over, and palaver, Rowley, Keith, &c. and Coffin to abuse the Earl! Now, I can tell you, that he is the Earl's spy.

It is Coffin, who has injured Sir Andrew Hammond so much: and his custom is, to abuse the Earl, to get people to speak out; and, then, the Earl takes his measures accordingly.

To me, it is nothing. Thank God! there can be no tales told of my cheating; or, I hope, neglecting my duty. Whilst I serve, I will serve well, and closely; when I want rest, I will go to Merton.

You know, my dear Emma, that I am never well when it blows hard. Therefore, imagine what a cruize off Toulon is; even in summer time, we have a hard gale every week, and two days heavy swell.

It would kill you; and myself, to see you. Much less possible, to have Charlotte, Horatia, &c. on board ship!

And I, that have given orders to carry no women to sea in the Victory, to be the first to break them!

And, as to Malta, I may never see it, unless we have an engagement; and, perhaps, not then: for, if it is complete, I may go home, for three months, to see you; but, if you was at Malta, I might absolutely miss you, by leaving the Mediterranean without warning.

The other day, we had a report the French were out, and seen steering to the westward. We were as far as Minorca, when the alarm proved false.

Therefore, my dearest beloved Emma! although I should be the happiest of men, to live and die with you, yet my chance of seeing you is much more certain by your remaining at Merton, than wandering where I may never go; and, certainly, never to stay forty-eight hours.

You cannot, I am sure, more ardently long to see me, than I do to be with you; and, if the war goes on, it is my intention to get leave to spend the next winter in England: but I verily believe that, long before that time, we shall have peace.

As for living in Italy, that is entirely out of the question. Nobody cares for us, there; and, if I had Bronte—which, thank God! I shall not—it would cost me a fortune to go there, and be tormented out of my life. I should never settle my affairs there.

I know, my own dear Emma, if she will let her reason have fair play, will say, I am right; but she is, like Horatia, very angry, if she cannot have her own way. Her Nelson is called upon, in the most honourable manner, to defend his country! Absence, to us, is equally painful: but, if I had either stayed at home, or neglected my duty abroad, would not my Emma have blushed for me? She could never have heard of my praises, and how the country looks up.

I am writing, my dear Emma, to reason the point with you; and, I am sure, you will see it in its true light. But I have said my say, on this subject, and will finish.

I have received your letter, with Lord William's and Mr. Kemble's, about Mr. Palmer: he is also recommended by the Duke of Clarence; and, he says, by desire of the Prince of Wales. I have, without him, twenty-six to be made Captains, and list every day increasing. It is not one whole French fleet that can get through it.

I shall, probably, offend many more than I can oblige. Such is always the case: like the tickets—those who get them, feel they have a right to them; and those [who] do not get them, feel offended for ever.

But, I cannot help it: I shall endeavour to do what is right, in every situation; and some ball may soon close all my accounts with this world of care and vexation!

But, never mind, my own dear-beloved Emma: if you are true to me, I care not—and approve of all my actions. However, as you say, I approve of them, myself; therefore, probably, I am right.

Poor Reverend Mr. Scott is, I fear, in a very bad way. His head has been turned by too much learning, and the stroke of lightning will never let him be right again. The Secretary Scott is a treasure; and I am very well mounted: Hardy is every thing I could wish or desire.

Our days pass so much alike that, having described one, you have them all. We now breakfast by candlelight; and all retire, at eight o'clock, to bed.

Naples, I fancy, is in a very bad way, in regard to money. They have not, or pretend not to have, enough to pay their officers; and, I verily believe, if Acton was to give up his place, that it would become a province of France. Only think of Buonaparte's writing to the Queen, to desire her influence to turn out Acton! She answered, properly: at least, so says Mr. Elliot, who knows more of Naples than any of us; God help him!—and General Acton has, I believe, more power than ever.

By Gibbs's letter, I see, he has sent over about my accounts at Bronte. He can have no interest in being unfriendly to me. Why should he? I want no great matters from him; and he can want nothing from me, that it is not my duty to give his Sovereigns: therefore, why should he be against us! For my part, my conduct will not alter, whether he is or not.

Our friend, Sir Alexander, is a very great diplomatic character; and, even an Admiral must not know what he is negotiating about: although you will scarcely believe, that the Bey of Tunis sent the man at my desire.

You shall judge—viz. "The Tunisian Envoy is still here, negotiating. He is a moderate man; and, apparently, the best disposed of any I ever did business with." Could even the oldest diplomatic character be drier? I hate such parade of nonsense! But, I will turn from such stuff.

You ask me, Do you do right to give Charlotte things? I shall only say, my dear Emma, whatever you do in that way, I shall always approve. I only wish, I had more power than I have! But, somehow, my mind was not sharp enough for prize-money. Lord Keith would have made twenty thousand pounds, and I have not made six thousand.

Poor Mr. Este, how I pity him! but, what shall I do with him? However, if he comes, I shall shew him all the kindness in my power.

October 22d.

The vessel is just going off. I have not a scrap of news! Only, be assured of my most affectionate regard.

Remember me kindly to Charlotte. Shall always love those that are good to Horatia. I will write her by another opportunity.

Remember me to Mrs. Cadogan.

You may be sure, I do not forget Charles, who has not been well; Captain Capel is very good to him.

I am, ever, for ever, my dearest Emma, your most faithful and affectionate

NELSON & BRONTE.

LETTER XL.

Victory, under Majorca,
January 13th, 1804.

MY OWN DEAR BELOVED EMMA,

I received, on the 9th, your letters of September 29th, October 2, 7, 10, 12, 17th, November 5th, 8th, to the 24th: and I am truly sensible of all your kindness and affectionate regard for me; which, I am sure, is reciprocal, in every respect, from your own Nelson.

If that Lady Bitch knew of that person's coming to her house, it was a trick; but which, I hope, you will not subject yourself to again. But, I do not like it!

However, it is passed; and, we must have confidence in each other: and, my dearest Emma, judging of you by myself, it is not all the world that could seduce me, in thought, word, or deed, from all my soul holds most dear.

Indeed, if I can help it, I never intend to go out of the ship, but to the shore of Portsmouth; and that will be, if it pleases God, before next Christmas. Indeed, I think, long before, if the French will venture to sea.

I send you a letter from the Queen of Naples. They call out, might and main, for our protection; and, God knows, they are sure of me.

Mr. Elliot complains heavily of the expence; and says, he will retire the moment it is peace. He expected his family, when they would sit down eleven Elliots!

If, my dear Emma, you are to mind all the reports you may hear, you may always be angry with your Nelson.

In the first place, instead of eight days, Mr. Acourt; he came on board one day, just before dinner, and left me next morning, after breakfast.

What pleasure people can have in telling lies! But, I care not what they say; I defy them all.

You may safely rely, that I can for ever repeat, with truth, these words—for ever I love you, and only you, my Emma; and, you may be assured, as long as you are the same to me, that you are never absent a moment from my thoughts.

I am glad you are going to Merton; you will live much more comfortable, and much cheaper, than in London: and this spring, if you like to have the house altered, you can do it. But, I fancy, you will soon tire of so much dirt, and the inconvenience will be very great the whole summer.

All I request, if you fix to have it done, [is] that Mr. Davison's architect, who drew the plan, may have the inspection; and, he must take care that it does not exceed the estimate.

If it is done by contract, you must not alter; or a bill is run-up, much worse than if we had never contracted. Therefore, I must either buy the materials, and employ respectable workmen, under the architect; or, contract.

I rather believe, it would be better for me to buy the materials, and put out the building to a workman; but, you must get some good advice.

With respect to the new entrance— * * * * * * * * * * * * *
* * * * * * * * * * *

LETTER XLI.

Victory, March 14th, [1804] off Toulon.

Young Faddy, my Dearest Emma, brought me, two days ago, your dear and most kind letter of November 26th, and you are sure that I shall take a very early opportunity of promoting him; and he appears to be grown a fine young man, but vacancies do not happen very frequently in this station. However, if he behaves well, he may be sure of me.

With respect to Mr. Jefferson, I can [neither] say nor do any thing. The surgeon of the Victory is a very able, excellent man, and the ship is kept in the most perfect state of health; and, I would not, if I could—but, thank [God] I cannot—do such an unjust act, as to remove him. He is my own asking for! and, I have every reason to be perfectly content.

Mr. Jefferson got on, by my help; and, by his own misconduct, he got out of a good employ, and has seen another person, at Malta hospital, put over his head. He must now begin again; and act with much more attention and sobriety, than he has done, to ever get forward again: but, time may do much; and, I shall rejoice to hear of his reformation.

I am not surprised, my dearest Emma, at the enormous expences of the watering place; but, if it has done my own Emma service, it is well laid out. A thousand pounds a year will not go far; and we need be great economists, to make both ends meet, and to carry on the little improvements. As for making one farthing more prize-money, I do not expect it; except, by taking the French fleet: and, the event of that day, who can foresee!

With respect to Mrs. Græfer—what she has done, God and herself knows; but I have made up my mind, that Gibbs will propose an hundred pounds a year for her: if so, I shall grant it, and have done. I send you Mrs. Græfer's last letter.

Whilst I am upon the subject of Bronte, I have one word more—and your good, dear, kind heart, must not think that I shall die one hour the sooner; on the contrary, my mind has been more content ever since I have done: I have left you a part of the rental of Bronte, to be first paid every half year, and in advance. It is but common justice; and, whether Mr. Addington gives you any thing, or not, you will want it.

I would not have you lay out more than is necessary, at Merton. The rooms, and the new entrance, will take a good deal of money. The entrance by the corner I would have certainly done; a common white gate will do for the present; and one of the cottages, which is in the barn, can be put up, as a temporary lodge. The road can be made to a temporary bridge; for that part of the Nile, one day, shall be filled up.

Downing's canvas awning will do for a passage. For the winter, the carriage can be put in the barn; and, giving up Mr. Bennett's premises, will save fifty pounds a year: and, another year, we can fit up the coach-house and stables, which are in the barn.

The foot-path should be turned. I did shew Mr. Haslewood the way I wished it done; and Mr. ——— will have no objections, if we make it better than ever it has been: and, I also beg, as my dear Horatia is to be at Merton, that a strong netting, about three feet high, may be placed round the Nile, that the little thing may not tumble in; and, then, you may have ducks again in it. I forget, at what place we saw the netting; and either Mr. Perry, or Mr. Goldsmid, told us where it was to be bought. I shall be very anxious until I know this is done.

I have had no very late opportunities of sending to Naples: but, viâ Malta, I wrote to Gibbs, to desire he would send over and purchase the amorins. They will arrive in time. I hope, the watch is arrived safe.

The British Fair cutter, I hope, is arrived safe. She has three packets, from me, to England,

The expences of the alterations at Merton you are not to pay from the income. Let it all be put to a separate account, and I will provide a fund for the payment.

All I long for, just now, is to hear that you are perfectly recovered; and, then, I care for nothing: all my hopes are, to see you, and be happy, at dear Merton, again; but, I fear, this miscarriage of Pichegru's, in France, will prolong the war. It has kept the French fleet in port, which we are all sorry for.

Sir William Bolton was on board yesterday. He looks thin. The fag in a brig is very great; and I see no prospect of his either making prize-money, or being made post, at present: but, I shall omit no opportunity.

I wrote to Mrs. Bolton a few months ago; and gave her letter, yesterday, to Bolton. He conducts himself very well, indeed.

Ever, my dearest Emma, for ever, I am your most faithful, and affectionate

NELSON & BRONTE.

Although I cannot well afford it, yet I could not bear that poor blind Mrs. Nelson should be in want in her old days, and sell her plate; therefore, if you will find out what are her debts, if they come within my power, I will certainly pay them.

Many, I dare say, if they had commanded here, would have made money; but, I can assure you, for prizes taken within the Mediterranean, I have not more than paid my expences. However, I would rather pinch myself, than she, poor soul, should want. Your good, angelic heart, my dearest beloved Emma, will fully agree with me, every thing is very expensive; and, even we find it, and will be obliged to economise, if we assist our friends: and, I am sure, we should feel more comfort in it than in loaded tables, and entertaining a set of people who care not for us.

An account is this moment brought me, that a small sum is payable to me, for some neutral taken off Cadiz in May 1800; so that I shall not be poorer for my gift. It is odd, is it not?

I shall, when I come home, settle four thousand pounds in trustees hands, for Horatia; for, I will not put it in my own power to have her left destitute: for she would want friends, if we left her in this world. She shall be independent of any smiles or frowns!

I am glad you are going to take her home; and, if you will take the trouble with Eliza and Ann, I am the very last to object.

Tom, I shall certainly assist at college; and, I am sure, the Doctor expects that I should do the same for Horace: but I must make my arrangements, so as not to run in debt.

April 9th.

I have wrote to the Duke; but, by your account, I fear he is not alive. I write, because you wish me; and, because I like the Duke, and hope he will leave you some money. But, for myself, I can have no right to expect a farthing: nor would I be a legacy hunter for the world; I never knew any good come from it.

I send you a letter from Mr. Falconet. I am afraid, they have made a jumble about the amorins. And I send you a very impertinent letter from that old cat. I have sent her a very dry answer, and told her, I should send the sweetmeats to you. I always hated the old bitch! But, was she young, and as beautiful as an angel, I am engaged; I am all, soul and body, my Emmas: nor would I change her for all this world could give me.

I would not have Horatia think of a dog. I shall not bring her one; and, I am sure, she is better without a pet of that sort. But, she is like her mother, would get all the old dogs in the place about her.

April 14th.

I am so sea-sick, that I cannot write another line; except, to say—God Almighty bless you, my dearest beloved Emma! prays, ever, your faithful

NELSON & BRONTE.

LETTER XLII.

Victory, April 2d, 1804.

I have, my Dearest Beloved Emma, been so uneasy for this last month; desiring, most ardently, to hear of your well doing!

Captain Capel brought me your letters, sent by the Thisbe, from Gibraltar. I opened—opened—found none but December, and early in January. I was in such an agitation! At last, I found one without a date: which, thank God! told my poor heart, that you was recovering; but, that dear little Emma was no more! and, that Horatia had been so very ill—it all together upset me.

But, it was just at bed-time; and I had time to reflect, and be thankful to God for sparing you and our dear Horatia. I am sure, the loss of one—much more, both—would have drove me mad. I was so agitated, as it was, that I was glad it was night, and that I could be by myself.

Kiss dear Horatia, for me: and tell her, to be a dutiful and good child; and, if she is, that we shall always love her.

You may, if you like, tell Mrs. G. that I shall certainly settle a small pension on her. It shall not be large, as we may have the pleasure of making her little presents; and, my dearest Emma, I shall not be wanting to every body who has been kind to you, be they servants or gentlefolks.

Admiral Lutwidge is a good man; and, I like Mrs. Lutwidge—and shall, always more, because she is fond of you.

Never mind the great Bashaw at the Priory. He be damned! If he was single, and had a mind to marry you, he could only make you a Marchioness: but, as he is situated, and I situated, I can make you a Duchess; and, if it pleases God, that time may arrive! Amen. Amen.

As for your friend Lady H——, she is, in her way, as great a pimp as any of them.

What a set! But, if they manage their own intrigues, is not that enough! I am sure, neither you or I care what they do; much less, envy them their chere amies.

As for Lord S——, and the other, I care nothing about them; for I have every reason, by my own feelings towards you, to think you care only for your Nelson.

I have not heard of your receiving the little box from Naples; bracelets, I fancy, but I did not open them.

I wish the amorins may come in time for the conveyance of Captain Layman; who has, most unfortunately, lost his sloop: he is strongly recommended, by the governor and garrison of Gibraltar. But, perhaps, he may not be able to obtain it.

We have such reports about the King's health, that the present ministry may be out; and, for what I know or care, another set may be no better, for you or me.

As for the Admiralty, let who will be in, they can neither do me any great good or harm: they may vex me, a little; but, that will recoil upon themselves.

I hope, however, they will confirm Captain Layman; for he is attached not only to me, but is a very active officer. But, it was his venturing to know more about India than Troubridge, that made them look shy upon him; and, his tongue runs too fast. I often tell him, not to let his tongue run so fast, or his pen write so much.

LETTER XLIII.

Victory, off Toulon,
April 10th, 1804.

MY DEAREST EMMA,

I have received all your truly kind and affectionate letters, to January 25th, by the Thisbe; and, last night, your letter of January 13th, by Naples.

The amorins will go under the care of Captain Layman; who, unfortunately, lost his sloop: but, with much credit to himself, he has been acquitted of all blame.

I rejoice that dear Horatia is got well; and, also, that you, my dearest Emma, are recovered of your severe indisposition.

In our present situation with Spain, this letter, probably, may never reach you. I have wrote fully; and intend to send them by the Argus, who I expect to join every minute.

Elphi Bey, I hear, has had all his fine things taken from him. He escaped into the Desert, and is pursued; probably, his head is off, long before this time.

The French fleet came out on the 5th, but went in again the next morning.

Yesterday, a Rear-Admiral, and seven sail of ships, including frigates, put their nose outside the harbour. If they go on playing this game, some day we shall lay salt upon their tails; and so end the campaign of, my dearest Emma, your most faithful and affectionate

———

I am glad to hear that you are going to take my dear Horatia, to educate her. She must turn out an angel, if she minds what you say to her; and Eliza and Ann will never forget your goodness.

My health is so, so! I shall get through the summer; and, in the winter, shall go home.

You will readily fancy all I would say, and do think.

My kind love to all friends.

LETTER XLIV.

Victory, April 19th, 1804.

MY DEAREST EMMA,

I had wrote you a line, intended for the Swift cutter; but, instead of her joining me, I had the mortification, not only to hear that she was taken, but that all the dispatches and letters had fallen into the hands of the enemy; a very pretty piece of work!

I am not surprised at the capture; but am very much so, that any dispatches should be sent in a vessel with twenty-three men, not equal to cope with any row-boat privateer.

As I do not know what letters of your's are in her, I cannot guess what will be said. I suppose, there will be a publication.

The loss of the Hindostan, was great enough; but, for importance, it is lost, in comparison to the probable knowledge the enemy will obtain of our connections with foreign countries! Foreigners for ever say—and it is true—"We dare not trust England; one way, or other, we are sure to be committed!" However, it is now too late to launch out on this subject.

Not a thing has been saved out of the Hindostan, not a second shirt for any one; and it has been by extraordinary exertions, that the people's lives were saved.

Captain Hallowell is so good as to take home, for me, wine as by the inclosed list; and, if I can, some honey. The Spanish honey is so precious, that if [any one has] a cut, or sore throat, it is used to cure it. I mention this, in case you should wish to give the Duke a jar. The smell is wonderful! It is to be produced no where, but in the mountains near Rosas.

The Cyprus wine, one hogshead, was for Buonaparte.

I would recommend the wine-cooper drawing it off: and you can send a few dozens to the Duke; who, I know, takes a glass every day at two o'clock.

I wish, I had any thing else to send you; but, my dearest Emma, you must take the will for the deed.

I am pleased with Charlotte's letter; and, as she loves my dear Horatia, I shall always like her.

What hearts those must have, who do not! But, thank God, she shall not be dependent on any of them.

Your letter of February 12th, through Mr. Falconet, I have received. I know, they are all read; therefore, never sign your name. I shall continue to write, through Spain; but never say a word that can convey any information—except, of eternal attachment and affection for you; and that, I care not, who knows; for I am, for ever, and ever, your, only your,

NELSON & BRONTE.

Poor Captain Le Gros had your note to him in his pocket-book, and that was all he saved.

Mr. Este left him at Gibraltar, and went to Malta in the Thisbe.

Captain Le Gros is now trying. I think, it will turn out, that every person is obliged to his conduct for saving their lives.

She took fire thirteen leagues from the land.

LETTER XLV.

Victory, April 23,1804.

MY DEAREST EMMA,

Hallowell has promised me, if the Admiralty will give him leave to go to London, that he will call at Merton.

His spirit is certainly more independent than almost any man's I ever knew; but, I believe, he is attached to me. I am sure, he has no reason to be so, to either Troubridge or any one at the Admiralty.

I have sent, last night, a box of Marischino Veritabile of Zara, which I got Jemmy Anderson to buy for me, and twelve bottles of tokay. I have kept none for myself, being better pleased that you should have it.

I am, ever, and for ever, your most faithful and affectionate

NELSON & BRONTE.

Hallowell parted last night; but, being in sight, I am sending a frigate with a letter to the Admiralty.

May God Almighty bless you, and send us a happy meeting!

LETTER XLVI.

Victory, May 5, 1804.

I find, my Dearest Emma, that your picture is very much admired by the French Consul at Barcelona; and that he has not sent it to be admired—which, I am sure, it would be—by Buonaparte.

They pretend, that there were three pictures taken. I wish, I had them: but they are all gone, as irretrievably as the dispatches; unless we may read them in a book, as we printed their correspondence from Egypt.

But, from us, what can they find out! That I love you, most dearly; and hate the French, most damnably.

Dr. Scott went to Barcelona, to try to get the private letters; but, I fancy, they are all gone to Paris. The Swedish and American Consuls told him, that the French Consul had your picture, and read your letters; and, Doctor thinks, one of them probably read the letters.

By the master's account of the cutter, I would not have trusted a pair of old shoes in her. He tells me, she did not sail, but was a good sea-boat.

I hope, Mr. Marsden will not trust any more of my private letters in such a conveyance; if they choose to trust the affairs of the public in such a thing, I cannot help it.

I long for the invasion being over; it must finish the war, and I have no fears for the event.

I do not say, all I wish; and which, my dearest beloved Emma—(read that, whoever opens this letter; and, for what I care, publish it to the world)—your fertile imagination can readily fancy I would say: but this I can say, with great truth, that I am, FOR EVER, YOUR'S

LETTER XLVII.

Victory, May 27th, 1804.

MY DEAREST EMMA,

Yesterday, I took Charles Connor on board, from the Phoebe, to try what we can do with him. At present, poor fellow, he has got a very bad eye—and, I almost fear, that he will be blind of it—owing to an olive-stone striking his eye: but the surgeon of the Victory, who is by far the most able medical man I have ever seen, and equally so as a surgeon, [says] that, if it can be saved, he will do it.

The other complaint, in his head, is but little more, I think, than it was when he first came to Deal; a kind of silly laugh, when spoken to. He always complains of a pain in the back part of his head; but, when that is gone, I do not perceive but that he is as wise as many of his neighbours.

You may rely, my dear Emma, that nothing shall be wanting, on my part, to render him every service.

Capel—although, I am sure, very kind to younkers—-I do not think, has the knack of keeping them in high discipline; he lets them be their own master too much.

I paid Charles's account, yesterday; since he has been in the Phoebe, one hundred and fifty-five pounds, fourteen shillings. However, he must now turn over a new leaf; and I sincerely hope, poor fellow, he will yet do well.

I wrote you on the 22d, through Rosas, in Spain; and I shall write, in a few days, by Barcelona: this goes by Gibraltar.

I have wrote Admiral Lutwidge; Mrs. Lutwidge must wait, for I cannot get through all my numerous letters: for, whoever writes, although upon their own affairs, are offended if they are not answered.

I have not seen young Bailey: I suppose, he is in the Leviathan. By the parcel, I see, he is in the Canopus; and I can, at present, be of no use to him.

May 30th.

Charles is very much recovered.

I write you, this day, by Barcelona. Your dear phiz—but not the least like you—on the cup, is safe: but I would not use it, for the world; for, if it was broke, it would distress me very much.

Your letters, by Swift, I shall never get back. The French Consul, at Barcelona, is bragging that he has three pictures of you from the Swift.

I do not believe him; but, what if he had a hundred! Your resemblance is so deeply engraved in my heart, that there it can never be effaced: and, who knows? some day, I may have the happiness of having a living picture of you!

Old Mother L—— is a damned b——: but I do not understand what you mean, or what plan.

I am not surprised at my friend Kingsmill admiring you, and forgetting Mary; he loves variety, and handsome women.

You touch upon the old Duke; but, I am dull of comprehension: believing you all my own, I cannot imagine any one else to offer, in any way.

We have enough, with prudence; and, without it, we should soon be beggars, if we had five times as much.

I see, Lord Stafford is going to oppose Mr. Addington; the present ministry cannot stand.

I wish Mr. Addington had given you the pension; Pitt, and hard-hearted Grenville, never will.

What a fortune the death of Lord Camelford gives him!

Every thing you tell me about my dear Horatia charms me. I think I see her, hear her, and admire her; but, she is like her dear, dear mother.

I am sorry, if your account of George Martin's wife is correct; he deserved a better fate. But, he is like Foley; gave up a great deal, to marry the relation of a great man: although, in fact, she is no relation to the Duke of Portland.

I wish, I could but be at dear Merton, to assist in making the alterations. I think, I should have persuaded you to have kept the pike, and a clear stream; and to have put all the carp, tench, and fish who muddy the water, into the pond. But, as you like, I am content. Only take care, that my darling does not fall in, and get drowned. I begged you to get the little netting along the edge; and, particularly, on the bridges.

I admire the seal; and God bless you, also! Amen.

The boy, South, is on board another ship, learning to be a musician. He will return soon, when he shall have the letter and money. I hope, he will deserve it; but he has been a very bad boy: but good floggings, I hope, will save him from the gallows.

Mr. Falcon is a clever man. He would not have made such a blunder as our friend Drake, and Spencer Smith. I hear, the last is coming, viâ Trieste, to Malta. Perhaps, he wants to get to Constantinople; and, if the Spencers get in, the Smiths will get any thing.

Mr. Elliot, I hear, is a candidate for it. He complains of the expence of Naples, I hear; and, that he cannot make both ends meet, although he sees no company.

The histories of the Queen are beyond whatever I have heard from Sir William. Prince Leopold's establishment is all French. The Queen's favourite, Lieutenant-Colonel St. Clair, was a subaltern; La Tour, the Captain in the navy; and, another!

However, I never touch on these matters; for, I care not how she amuses herself.

It will be the upset of Acton; or, rather, he will not, I am told, stay.

The King is angry with her; his love is long gone by.

I have only one word more—Do not believe a syllable the newspapers say, or what you hear. Mankind seems fond of telling lies.

Remember me kindly to Mrs. Cadogan, and all our mutual friends; and be assured, I am, for ever, my dearest Emma, your most faithful and affectionate

NELSON & BRONTE.

George Campbell desires me always to present his best respects; and make mine to good Mr. Yonge. What can I write him? I am sure, he must have great pleasure in attending you: and, when you see Sir William Scott, make my best regards acceptable to him. There is no man I have a higher opinion of, both as a public and private character.

You will long ago have had my letter; with one to Davison, desiring he will pay for the alterations at Merton. I shall send you a letter for the hundred pounds a month, to the Bank.

LETTER XLVIII.

Victory, June 6th, 1804.

Since I wrote you, my Dearest Emma, on the 30th and 31st May, nothing new has happened; except our hearing the feu de joie at Toulon, for the declaration of Emperor.

What a capricious nation those French must be! However, I think it must, in any way, be advantageous to England. There ends, for a century, all republics!

By vessels from Marseilles, the French think it will be a peace; and they say, that several of their merchant ships are fitting out. I earnestly pray, that it may be so; and, that we may have a few years of rest.

I rather believe, my antagonist at Toulon, begins to be angry with me: at least, I am trying to make him so; and then, he may come out, and beat me, as he says he did, off Boulogne.

He is the Admiral that went to Naples in December 1792, La Touche Treville, who landed the grenadiers. I owe him something for that.

I am better, my dear Emma, than I have been, and shall get through the summer very well; and I have the pleasure to tell you, that Charles is very much recovered. There is no more the matter with his intellects, than with mine! Quite the contrary; he is very quick.

Mr. Scott, who has overlooked all his things, says, his clothes, &c. are in the highest order he has ever seen.

I shall place him in the Niger, with Captain Hilliar, when he joins; but, all our ships are so full, that it is very difficult to get a birth for one in any ship.

Would you conceive it possible! but, it is now from April 2d, since I have heard direct from Ball. The average time for a frigate to go, and return, is from six to seven weeks.

From you, I had letters, April 5th, and the papers to April 8th, received May 10th, with a convoy.

This goes through friend Gayner.

Sir William Bolton joined last night; and received his letters, announcing his being called papa. He is got a very fine young man and good officer.

Lord St. Vincent has desired he may have the first Admiralty vacancy for post; but nobody will die, or go home.

A-propos! I believe, you should buy a piece of plate, value fifty pounds, for our god-daughter of Lady Bolton; and something of twenty or thirty pounds value, for Colonel Suckling's.

But, my Emma, you are not to pay for them, let it rest for me; or, if the amount is sent me, I will order payment.

Remember me most kindly to Horatia, good Mrs. Cadogan, Charlotte, Miss Connor, and all our friends at dear, dear Merton; where, from my soul, I wish I was, this moment: then, I sincerely hope, we should have no cause for sorrow.

You will say what is right to Mr. Perry, Newton, Patterson, Mr. Lancaster, &c. you know all these matters. God in Heaven bless and preserve you, for ever! prays, ever, your's most faithfully,

---

LETTER XLIX.

Victory, June 10th, 1804.

MY DEAREST EMMA,

I wrote to you, on the 6th, viâ Rosas: this goes by Barcelona; to which place I am sending Sir William Bolton, to fetch Dr. Scott, who is gone there, poor fellow, for the benefit of his health!

I have just had very melancholy letters from the King and Queen of Naples, on account of General Acton's going to Sicily.

The insolence of Buonaparte was not to be parried without a war; for which they are unable, if unassisted.

I have letters from Acton, May 28, on board the Archimedes, just going into Palermo. He will probably return to Naples, unless new events arise: and that may be; for a minister, once out, may find some difficulty in renewing his post. He has acted with great and becoming spirit.

I am better, but I have been very unwell. It blows, here, as much as ever. Yesterday was a little hurricane of wind.

I dare say, Prince Castelcicala knows it by express; if not, you may tell him, with my best respects. He, and every one else, may be sure of my attachment to those good sovereigns. By this route, I do not choose to say more on this subject.

With my kindest regards to Horatia and your good mother, Charlotte, Miss C. and all our friends, believe me, my dear Emma, for ever, your most faithful and affectionate

---

I fear, Sardinia will be invaded from Corsica before you get this letter. I have not small ships to send there, or any where else; not in the proportion of one to five.

You may communicate this to Mr. Addington, if you think that he does not know it; but, to no one else, except Castelcicala, of what relates to Naples.

I have very flattering letters from the Grand Vizier, in the name of the Sultan; and from Cadir, now Capitan Pacha.

LETTER L.

Victory, July 1st, 1804.

Although I have wrote you, my dearest Emma, a letter, by Rosas, of June 27th, not yet gone, the weather being so very bad, that ships cannot get across the Gulph of Lyons, yet I will [not] miss the opportunity of writing by Gibraltar.

You must not, my Emma, think of hearing from me by way of Malta; it takes as long to send a letter to Malta, as to England.

The Monmouth, which you complain of not hearing by, I knew nothing of her movements for some months before. The ships from Malta, with the convoys, pick up our letters at Gibraltar. Therefore, do not hurt my feelings, by telling me that I neglect any opportunity of writing.

Your letters of April 13th, 22d, and May 13th, through Mr. Falconet, came safe, a few days ago. Mr. Falconet is the French banker; and he dare not buy a little macaroni for me, or let an Englishman into his house.

Gibbs is still at Palermo: I fancy, he will make a good thing of my estate; however, I wish it was settled. He wrote me, a short time since, that he wished I would give him a hint (but without noticing that it came from him) that I thought Mrs. Græfer and her child had better go to England; on pretence of educating her daughter, &c.

But I would have nothing to do with any such recommendation. It would end in her coming to me, in England; and saying, that she could not live upon what she had, and that I advised her to come to England, or she should not have thought of it.

In short, Gibbs wants to remove her. He is afraid of his pocket, I fancy; and the daughter is, I fancy, now in some seminary at Palermo, at Gibbs's expence.

I wrote him word, fully, I would advise no such thing; she was to form her own judgment.

What our friends are after at Naples, they best know. The poor King is miserable at the loss of Acton.

The Queen writes me about honest Acton, &c. &c. and I hear, that she has been the cause of ousting him: and they say—her enemies—that her conduct is all French. That, I do not believe; although she is likely to be the dupe of French emigrés, who always beset her.

I doubt much, my dear Emma, even her constancy of real friendship to you; although, in my letter to Acton, which Mr. Elliot says he read to her, I mentioned the obligations she was under to you, &c. &c. in very strong terms.

What could the name of the minister signify! It was the letter which was wanted to the Prime-Minister.

But, never mind; with prudence, we shall do very well.

I have wrote to Davison, by land: who, I am very sorry for; but, he never would take a friend's caution, and he has been severely bit.

Your accounts of Merton delight me; and you will long ago have known, that I have directed the bills for the alterations to be paid. I never could have intended to have taken it from the hundred pounds a month.

You will not hear of my making prize-money. I have not paid my expences these last nine months.

I shall expect to eat my Christmas dinner at Merton; unless those events happen which I can neither foresee nor prevent.

I am not well: and must have rest, for a few months, even should the country [want me;] which, very likely, they will not. News, I can have none. April 9th, Leviathan sailed; so government don't care much for us.

Kiss my dear Horatia, for me! I hope you will have her at Merton; and, believe me, my dear Emma, that I am, for ever, as ever, your attached, faithful, and affectionate,

NELSON & BRONTE.

LETTER LI.

Victory, August 12th, 1804.

Although, my Dearest Emma, from the length of time my other letters have been getting to you, I cannot expect that this will share a better fate; yet, as the Childers is going to Rosas, to get us some news from Paris—which is the only way I know of what is passing in England—I take my chance of the post: but, I expect the Kent will be in England before this letter; and by which ship I write to the Admiralty relative to my health.

Therefore, I shall only say, that I hope a little of your good nursing, with ass's milk, will set me up for another campaign; should the Admiralty wish me to return, in the spring, for another year: but, I own, I think we shall have peace.

The Ambuscade arrived this day fortnight, with our victuallers, &c. and very acceptable they were. By her, I received your letters of May 14th, 22d, and 30th, viâ Lisbon; and, of April 9th, 18, 15th, May 10th, 18th, 29th, June 1st, 5th, through, I suppose, the Admiralty.

The box you mention, is not arrived; nor have I a scrap of a pen from Davison. The weather in the Mediterranean seems much altered. In July, seventeen days the fleet was in a gale of wind.

I have often wrote to Davison, to pay for all the improvements at Merton. The new-building the chamber over the dining-room, you must consider. The stair window, we settled, was not to be stopped up. The underground passage will, I hope, be made; but I shall, please God, soon see it all.

I have wrote you, my dear Emma, about Horatia; but, by the Kent, I shall write fully. May God bless you, my dearest best-beloved Emma! and believe me, ever, your most faithful and affectionate

---

Kind love, and regards, to Mrs. Cadogan, and all friends. God bless you, again and again!

LETTER LII.

Victory, August 20th, 1804.

MY DEAREST EMMA,

The Kent left us three days ago; and, as the wind has been perfectly fair since her departure, I think she will have a very quick passage, and arrive long before this letter. But, as a ship is going to Rosas, I will not omit the opportunity of writing through Spain; as, you say, the letters all arrive safe.

We have nothing but gales of wind; and I have had, for two days, fires in the cabin, to keep out the very damp air.

I still hope that, by the time of my arrival in England, we shall have peace. God send it!

I have not yet received your muff; I think, probably, I shall bring it with me.

I hope, Davison has done the needful, in paying for the alterations at Merton. If not, it is now too late; and we will fix a complete plan, and execute it next summer. I shall be clear of debt, and what I have will be my own.

God bless you! Amen. Amen.

George Elliot goes to Malta, for a convoy to England, this day. If you ever see Lord Minto, say so.

LETTER LIII.

Victory, August 31st, 1804—Say 30th, at Evening. Therefore, I wrote, in fact, this Day, through Spain.

MY EVER DEAREST EMMA,

Yesterday, I wrote to you, through Spain; this goes by Naples. Mr. Falconet, I think, will send it; although, I am sure, he feels great fear from the French minister, for having any thing to do with us.

Mr. Greville is a shabby fellow! It never could have been the intention of Sir William, but that you should have had seven hundred pounds a year neat money; for, when he made the will, the Income Tax was double to what it is at present; and the estate which it is paid from is increasing every year in value.

It may be law, but it is not just; nor in equity would, I believe, be considered as the will and intention of Sir William. Never mind! Thank God, you do not want any of his kindness; nor will he give you justice.

I may fairly say all this; because my actions are different, even to a person who has treated me so ill.

As to ———, I know the full extent of the obligation I owe him, and he may be useful to me again; but I can never forget his unkindness to you.

But, I guess, many reasons influenced his conduct, in bragging of his riches, and my honourable poverty; but, as I have often said, and with honest pride, what I have is my own; it never cost the widow a tear, or the nation a farthing.

I got what I have with my pure blood, from the enemies of my country. Our house, my own Emma, is built upon a solid foundation; and will last to us, when his house and lands may belong to others than his children.

I would not have believed it, from any one but you! But, if ever I go abroad again, matters shall be settled very differently.

I am working hard with Gibbs about Bronte, but the calls upon me are very heavy. Next September, I shall be clear; I mean, September 1805.

I have wrote to both Acton and the Queen about you. I do not think she likes Mr. Elliot; and, therefore, I wish she had never shewn him my letters about you. We also know, that he has a card of his own to play.

Dr. Scott, who is a good man—although, poor fellow! very often wrong in the head—is going with Staines, in, the Cameleon, just to take a peep at Naples and Palermo. I have introduced him to Acton, who is very civil to every body from me.

The Admiralty proceedings towards me, you will know much sooner than I shall. I hope they will do the thing, handsomely, and allow of my return in the spring; but, I do not expect it.

I am very uneasy at your and Horatia being on the coast: for you cannot move, if the French make the attempt; which, I am told, they have done, and been repulsed. Pray God, it may be true!

I shall rejoice to hear you and Horatia are safe at Merton; and happy shall I be, the day I join you. Gannam Justem.

Gaetano is very grateful for your remembrance of him. Mr. Chevalier is an excellent servant. William says, he has wrote twice; I suppose, he thinks that enough.

This is written within three miles of the fleet in Toulon, who are looking very tempting. Kind regards to Mrs. Cadogan, Charlotte, &c. and compliments to all our joint friends; for they are no friends of mine, who are not friends to Emma.

God bless you, again and again!

Captain Hardy has not been very well: and, I fancy, Admiral Murray will not be sorry to see England; especially, since he has been promoted * * * * * * * * * * * * * he expects his flag may get up.

God bless you, my dearest Emma; and, be assured, I am ever most faithfully your's.

LETTER LIV.

Victory, September 29th, 1804.

This day, my dearest Emma, which gave me birth, I consider as more fortunate than common days; as, by my coming into this world, it has brought me so intimately acquainted with you, who my soul holds most dear. I well know that you will keep it, and have my dear Horatia to drink my health. Forty-six years of toil and trouble! How few more, the common lot of mankind leads us to expect; and, therefore, it is almost time to think of spending the few last years in peace and quietness!

By this time, I should think, either my successor is named, or permission is granted me to come home; and, if so, you will not long receive this letter before I make my appearance: which will make us, I am sure, both truly happy.

We have had nothing, for this fortnight, but gales of easterly winds, and heavy rains; not a vessel of any kind, or sort, joined the fleet.

I was in hopes Dr. Scott would have returned from Naples; and that I could have told you something comfortable for you, from that quarter: and it is now seven weeks since we heard from Malta. Therefore, I know nothing of what is passing in the world.

I would not have you, my dear Emma, allow the work of brick and mortar to go on in the winter months. It can all be finished next summer; when, I hope, we shall have peace, or such an universal war as will upset that vagabond, Buonaparte.

I have been tolerable well, till this last bad weather, which has given me pains in my breast; but, never mind, all will be well when I get to Merton.

Admiral Campbell, who is on board, desires to be remembered to you. He does not like much to stay here, after my departure. Indeed, we all draw so well together in the fleet, that I flatter myself the sorrow for my departure will be pretty general.

Admiral Murray will be glad to get home; Hardy is as good as ever; and
 Mr. Secretary Scott is an excellent man.

God bless you, my dearest Emma! and, be assured, I am ever your most faithful and affectionate

N. & B.

Kiss dear Horatia. I hope she is at Merton, fixed.

LETTER LV.

Victory, October 7, [1804.] 2 P.M.

I wrote you, my Dearest Emma, this morning, by way of Lisbon; but a boat, which is going to Torbay, having brought out a cargo of potatoes, will I think get home before the Lisbon packet. I shall only say—Guzelle Gannam Justem—and that I love you beyond all the world! This may be read by French, Dutch, Spanish, or Englishmen; for it comes from the heart of, my Emma, your faithful and affectionate

NELSON & BRONTE.

I think the gentry will soon come out. I cannot say more by such a conveyance.

LETTER LVI.

Victory, October 13, 1804.

MY DEAREST EMMA,

The dreadful effects of the yellow fever, at Gibraltar, and many parts of Spain, will naturally give you much uneasiness; till you hear that, thank God, we are entirely free from it, and in the most perfect health, not one man being ill in the fleet. The cold weather will, I hope, cure the disorder.

Whilst I am writing this letter, a cutter is arrived from England with strong indications of a Spanish war.

I hope, from my heart, that it will not prove one. But, however that is, my die is cast; and, long before this time, I expect, another Admiral is far on his way to supersede me. Lord Keith, I think a very likely man.

I should, for your sake, and for many of our friends, have liked an odd hundred thousand pounds; but, never mind. If they give me the choice of staying a few months longer, it will be very handsome; and, for the sake of others, we would give up, my dear Emma, very much of our own felicity. If they do not, we shall be happy with each other, and with dear Horatia.

The cutter returns with my answers directly; therefore, my own Emma, you must only fancy all my thoughts and feelings towards you. They are every thing which a fond heart can fancy.

I have not a moment; I am writing and signing orders, whilst I am writing to my own Emma.

My life, my soul, God in Heaven bless you!

Your letter is September 16th, your last is August 27th.

I have not made myself understood, about Mrs. Bolton's money. You give away too much.

Kiss our dear Horatia a thousand times, for your own faithful Nelson. I send two hundred pounds, keep it for your own pocket money.

You must tell Davison, and Haslewood, that I cannot answer their letters. Linton cannot be fixed; but you will know whether I come home, or stay, from Mr. Marsden.

God bless you!

Tell my brother, that I have made Mr. Yonge a Lieutenant, into the Sea-horse frigate, Captain Boyle.

Once more, God bless my dearest Emma!

Write your name on the back of the bill, if you send any person for the money.

I have scrawled three lines to Davison, that he should not think I neglected him in his confinement.

I have received the inclosed from Allen. Can we assist the poor foolish man with a character?

LETTER LVII.

Victory, November 23,1804.

As all our communication with Spain is at an end, I can now only expect to hear from my own dear Emma by the very slow mode of Admiralty vessels, and it is now more than two months since the John Bull sailed.

I much fear, something has been taken; for they never would, I am sure, have kept me so long in the dark. However, by management, and a portion of good luck, I got the account from Madrid in a much shorter space of time than I could have hoped for; and I have set the whole Mediterranean to work, and think the fleet cannot fail of being successful: and, if I had had the spare troops at Malta at my disposal, Minorca would at this moment have had English colours flying.

This letter, my dearest beloved Emma, goes—although in Mr. Marsden's letter—such a roundabout way, that I cannot say all that my heart wishes. Imagine everything which is kind and affectionate, and you will come near the mark.

Where is my successor? I am not a little surprised at his not arriving! A Spanish war, I thought, would have hastened him. Ministers could not have thought that I wanted to fly the service, my whole life has proved the contrary; and, if they refuse me now: I shall most certainly leave this country in March or April; for a few months rest I must have, very soon. If I am in my grave, what are the mines of Peru to me!

But, to say the truth, I have no idea of killing myself. I may, with care, live yet to do good service to the state. My cough is very bad; and my side, where I was struck on the 14th of February, is very much swelled; at times, a lump as large as my fist, brought on, occasionally, by violent coughing: but, I hope, and believe, my lungs are yet safe.

Sir William Bolton is just arrived from Malta. I am preparing to send him a cruise, where he will have the best chance I can give him of making ten thousand pounds. He is a very attentive, good, young man.

I have not heard from Naples this age. I have, in fact, no small craft to send for news.

If I am soon to go home, I shall be with you before this letter.

May God bless you!

Thomson desires to be most kindly remembered to his dear wife and children. He is most sincerely attached to them; and wishes to save what he can for their benefit.

As our means of communicating are cut off, I have only to beg that you will not believe the idle rumours of battles, &c. &c. &c.

May Heavens bless you! prays, fervently, my dear Emma, ever your most faithful and affectionate

NELSON & BRONTE.

LETTER LVIII.

Victory, March 9th, 1805.

I do assure you, my Dearest Emma, that nothing can be more miserable, or unhappy, than your poor Nelson.

From the 19th of February, have we been beating from Malta to off Palma; where I am now anchored, the wind and sea being so very contrary and bad. But I cannot help myself, and no one in the fleet can feel what I do: and, to mend my fate, yesterday Captain Layman arrived—to my great surprise—not in his brig, but in a Spanish cartel; he having been wrecked off Cadiz, and lost all the dispatches and letters.

You will conceive my disappointment! It is now from November 2d, that I have had a line from England.

Captain Layman says—he is sure the letters are sunk, never to rise again; but, as they were not thrown overboard until the vessel struck the rock, I have much fear that they may have fallen into the hands of the Dons.

My reports from off Toulon, state the French fleet as still in port; but, I shall ever be uneasy at not having fallen in with them.

I know, my dear Emma, that it is in vain to repine; but my feelings are alive to meeting those fellows, after near two years hard service.

What a time! I could not have thought it possible that I should have been so long absent; unwell, and uncomfortable, in many respects.

However, when I calculate upon the French fleet's not coming to sea for this summer, I shall certainly go for dear England, and a thousand [times] dearer Merton. May Heavens bless you, my own Emma!

I cannot think where Sir William Bolton is got to; he ought to have joined me, before this time.

I send you a trifle, for a birth-day's gift. I would to God, I could give you more; but, I have it not!

I get no prize-money worth naming; but, if I have the good fortune to meet the French fleet, I hope they will make me amends for all my anxiety; which has been, and is, indescribable.

How is my dear Horatia? I hope you have her under your guardian wing, at Merton. May God bless her!

Captain Layman is now upon his trial. I hope he will come clear, with honour. I fear, it was too great confidence in his own judgment that got him into the scrape; but it was impossible that any person living could have exerted himself more, when in a most trying and difficult situation.

 March 10th.

Poor Captain L. has been censured by the court: but, I have my own opinion. I sincerely pity him; and have wrote to Lord Melville, and Sir Evan Nepean, to try what can be done. All together, I am much unhinged.

To-morrow, if the wind lasts, I shall be off Toulon.

Sir William Bolton is safe, I heard of him this morning. I hear, that a ship is coming out for him; but, as this is only rumour, I cannot keep him from this opportunity of being made post: and, I dare say, he will cause, by his delay, such a tumble, that Louis's son, who I have appointed to the Childers, will lose his promotion; and, then Sir Billy will be wished at the devil! But, I have done with this subject; the whole history has hurt me. Hardy has talked enough to him, to rouze his lethargic disposition.

I have been much hurt at the loss of poor Mr. Girdlestone! He was a good man; but there will be an end of us all.

What has Charles Connor been about? His is a curious letter! If he does not drink, he will do very well. Captain Hilliar has been very good to him.

Colonel Suckling, I find, has sent his son to the Mediterranean; taking him from the Narcissus, where I had been at so much pains to place him. I know not where to find a frigate to place him. He never will be so well and properly situated again. I am more plagued with other people's business, or rather nonsense, than with my own concerns,

With some difficulty, I have got Suckling placed in the Ambuscade, with Captain Durban, who came on board at the moment I was writing.

  March 31st.

The history of Suckling will never be done. I have this moment got from him your letter, and one from his father. I shall say nothing to him; I don't blame the child, but those who took [him] out of the most desirable situation in the navy. He never will get into such another advantageous ship: but, his father is a fool; and so, my dear Emma, that ends.

The box which you sent me in May 1804, is just arrived in the Diligent store-ship.

I have sent the arms to Palermo, to Gibbs. The clothes are very acceptable; I will give you a kiss, for sending them.

God bless you! Amen.

 April 1st.

I am not surprised that we should both think the same about the kitchen; and, if I can afford it, I should like it to be done: but, by the fatal example of poor Mr. Hamilton, and many others, we must take care not to get into debt; for, then, we can neither help any of our relations, and [must] be for ever in misery! But, of this, we [will] talk more, when we walk upon the poop at Merton.

Do you ever see Admiral and Mrs. Lutwidge? You will not forget me when you do.

To Mrs. Cadogan, say every thing that is kind; and to all our other friends: and, be assured, I am, for ever and ever, your's, and only your's,

 NELSON & BRONTE.

As I know that all the Mediterranean letters are cut and smoaked, and perhaps read, I do not send you a little letter in this; but your utmost stretch of fancy cannot imagine more than I feel towards my own dear Emma.

God bless you! Amen.

LETTER LIX.

Victory, off Plymouth, September 17th, [1805.] Nine o'Clock in the Morning. Blowing fresh at W.S.W. dead foul wind.

I sent, my own Dearest Emma, a letter for you, last night, in a Torbay boat, and gave the man a guinea to put it in the Post-Office.

We have had a nasty blowing night, and it looks very dirty.

I am now signalizing the ships at Plymouth to join me; but, I rather doubt their ability to get to sea. However, I have got clear of Portland, and have Cawsand Bay and Torbay under the lee.

I intreat, my dear Emma, that you will chear up; and we will look forward to many, many happy years, and be surrounded by our children's children. God Almighty can, when he pleases, remove the impediment.

My heart and soul is with you and Horatia.

I got this line ready, in case a boat should get alongside.

For ever, ever, I am your's, most devotedly,

NELSON & BRONTE.

Mr. Rose said, he would write to Mr. Bolton, if I was sailed; but, I have forgot to give him the direction: but I will send it, to-day. I think, I shall succeed very soon, if not at this moment.

Wednesday, September 18th, off the Lizard.

I had no opportunity of sending your letter yesterday, nor do I see any prospect at present. The Ajax and Thunderer are joining; but, it is nearly calm, with a swell from the westward. Perseverance has got us thus far; and the same will, I dare say, get us on.

Thomas seems to do very well, and content.

Tell Mr. Lancaster, that I have no doubt that his son will do very well.

God bless you, my own Emma!

I am giving my letters to Blackwood, to put on board the first vessel he meets going to England, or Ireland.

Once more, Heavens bless you! Ever, for ever, your

NELSON & BRONTE.

LETTER LX.

Victory, October 1st, 1805.

MY DEAREST EMMA,

It is a relief to me, to take up the pen, and write you a line; for I have had, about four o'clock this morning, one of my dreadful spasms, which has almost enervated me.

It is very odd! I was hardly ever better than yesterday. Freemantle stayed with me till eight o'clock, and I slept uncommonly well; but, was awoke with this disorder. My opinion of its effect, some one day, has never altered. However, it is entirely gone off, and I am only quite weak. The good people of England will not believe, that rest of body and mind is necessary for me! But, perhaps, this spasm may not come again these six months. I had been writing seven hours yesterday; perhaps, that had some hand in bringing it upon me.

I joined the fleet late on the evening of the 28th of September, but could not communicate with them until the next morning.

I believe, my arrival was most welcome; not only to the commander of the fleet, but also to every individual in it: and, when I came to explain to them the Nelson touch, it was like an electric shock. Some shed tears, all approved—"It was new, it was singular, it was simple!" and, from Admirals downwards, it was repeated—"It must succeed, if ever they will allow us to get at them! You are, my Lord, surrounded by friends whom you inspire with confidence." Some may be Judas's; but the majority are certainly much

pleased with my commanding them. * * * * * * * * * * * *
* * * * * * * * * *

SUPPLEMENT.

INTERESTING LETTERS, ELUCIDATORY OF Lord Nelson's Letters TO LADY HAMILTON,&c.

LETTERS FROM LORD NELSON,TO MISS HORATIA NELSON THOMSON,NOW MISS HORATIA NELSON, (Lord Nelson's Adopted Daughter;) AND MISS CHARLOTTE NELSON, (Daughter of the present Earl.)

Letters OF LORD NELSON, &c. TO MISS HORATIA NELSON THOMSON.

Victory, April 13th, 1804.

MY DEAR HORATIA,

I send you twelve books of Spanish dresses, which you will let your guardian angel, Lady Hamilton, keep for you, when you are tired of looking at them. I am very glad to hear, that you are perfectly recovered; and, that you are a very good child. I beg, my dear Horatia, that you will always continue so; which will be a great comfort to your most affectionate

NELSON & BRONTE.

TO MISS CHARLOTTE NELSON.

Victory, April 19th, 1804.

MY DEAR CHARLOTTE,

I thank you very much for your kind letters of January 3d, and 4th; and I feel truly sensible of your kind regard for that dear little orphan, Horatia.

Although her parents are lost; yet, she is not without a fortune: and, I shall cherish her to the last moment of my life; and curse them who curse her, and Heaven bless them who bless her! Dear innocent! she can have injured no one.

I am glad to hear, that she is attached to you; and, if she takes after her parents, so she will, to those who are kind to her.

I am, ever, dear Charlotte, your affectionate uncle,

NELSON & BRONTE.

LETTERS FROM ALEXANDER DAVISON, ESQ. TO LADY HAMILTON.

LETTERS OF ALEX. DAVISON, ESQ. &c.

I.

[1804.]

MY DEAR MADAM,

I have, equally with yourself, felt extremely uneasy all night, thinking on the letter, which is a very serious one; and, until we receive our next dispatches, I shall still feel every day more and more anxious.

I rely on that kind Providence, which has hitherto sheltered him under every danger, upon the occasion.

He was on the eve of engaging, for protection—and preservation—It is, indeed, an anxious moment!

I have long thought, a plan was in agitation regarding the Toulon fleet being given up; but, whether it was in contemplation at the period the last letter was written, I know not. I am rather disposed to think otherwise.

The next packet will explain the whole; and, I trust, will relieve our minds of that burden, hardly supportable at present.

I shall, this evening, go quietly into the country, and return to town about noon to-morrow: as I require air, and a little relaxation; for I am, actually, overpowered with business.

Your's, most truly,
    ALEX. DAVISON.
Thursday Morning.

II.

[1804,]

MY DEAR MADAM,

Yesterday, I wrote to you just in time to save the post: but, whether that letter, or even this, reach you, I have my doubts—if they do not, you have only yourself to blame; for I cannot, for the soul of me, make out the name of the place. You have been in such a hurry, when writing it, that it really is not legible; and I do not sufficiently know Norfolk, to guess at it.

I did yesterday, as I shall this—imitate your writing, leaving it to the Post-Office gentlemen to find it out.

I acquainted you, that I would take care to obey your wishes, and hold back your check on Coutts and Co. till such time as it would be quite convenient to yourself, and you tell me to send it for payment.

Your mind may be perfectly at ease on that score: as, indeed, it may in every thing in which you have to do with me—though we do, now and then, differ a little in trifles; but, not in essentials: having one, only one, object in mind, that of the comforts, and ultimate happiness, of our dear—your beloved Nelson; for whom, what would you or I not do?

What a world of matter is now in agitation! Every thing is big with events; and soon, very soon, I hope to see—what I have long desired, and anxiously [been] waiting for—an event to contribute to the glory, the independency, of our Nelson.

I still hope, ere Christmas, to see him: that hope founded on the darling expectation of his squadron falling in with a rich Spanish flotilla. I think, too, that the French fleet will now come out.

I have written to our dear friend every information I have been able to collect, and have sent him a continuation of all the newspapers.

It affords me particular pleasure, to hear you feel so happy in Norfolk. How is it possible it can be otherwise! seated, as you are, in the midst of the friends of your best friend; enjoying every kindness and attention in their power to shew to the favourite of their brother.

I shall be very much rejoiced, when you come back, to talk over very interesting objects which our dear friend will now have to pursue.

My best respects to your fire-side; and believe me, most sincerely, your's,

ALEX. DAVISON.

III.

Saturday, 22d September 1804.

MY DEAR MADAM,

Ever obedient to your lawful commands, I have implicitly obeyed your orders, in the purchase, this morning, of Messrs. Branscomb and Co. four quarter lottery-tickets—

{ No. 593.} { 10,376.} { 14,381.} { 20,457.}

Each, I hope, will come up prize; and be entitled to receive, at least, on the whole, twenty thousand pounds! I paid eighteen pounds eight shillings for them; and I have written upon the back of each—"Property of Lord Nelson, 22d September 1804. A.D."

When I have the pleasure of seeing you, I shall deliver the trust over to you, to receive the bespoken said sum of twenty thousand pounds. What a glorious receipt will it be!

I am glad you received my letters, though I could not make out the name of the place; the Post-Office runners are expert at it.

What do you say to a Spanish war? I think, now, the breeze begins to freshen; and that the flames, at last, will succeed.

I sent off, last night, a very long epistle to our dear Nelson. I am truly distressed at his not receiving my letters; though I can pretty well guess how to account for it, and in whose hands they were detained. Experience teaches us how better to guard against similar misfortunes; and, in future, I shall be cautious to whom I give my letters.

So that I know the Hero of heroes is well, I care the less about letters; knowing that writing, delivering, or receiving them, will not, either in him or me, make the least alteration, or lessen our attachment or affection.

I am pleased to see how happy you are in Norfolk. I wish you may not find it so fascinating, that the arrival of "Lord Nelson" at Merton would not induce you to [quit] the county!!!

I beg you will make my best respects acceptable to every friend (real) of that invaluable man, Lord Nelson.

   Your's, most truly,
     ALEX. DAVISON.

Letter from Lady Hamilton TO ALEXANDER DAVISON, ESQ. INCLOSING Her Ladyship's Verses on Lord Nelson.

Letter OF Lady Hamilton, &c.

Clarges Street,
[26th January 1805.]

I have been very ill, my Dear Sir; and am in bed with a cold, very bad cold indeed! But, the moment I am better, I will call on you.

I am invited to dine with Mr. Haslewood to-morrow, but fear I shall not be able to go.

I am very anxious about letters; but Admiral Campbell has told me, he thinks my dear Lord will soon be at home. God grant! for, I think, he might remove that stumbling-block, Sir John O! Devil take him!

That Polyphemus should have been Nelson's: but, he is rich in great and noble deeds; which t'other, poor devil! is not. So, let dirty wretches get pelf, to comfort them; victory belongs to Nelson. Not, but what I think money necessary for comforts; and, I hope, our, your's, and my Nelson, will get a little, for all Master O.

I write from bed; and you will see I do, by my scrawl.

I send you some of my bad Verses on my soul's Idol.

God bless you! Remember, you will soon be free; and let that cheer you, that you will come out with even more friends than ever. I can only say, I am your ever obliged, and grateful,

 EMMA HAMILTON.

I long to see and know Nepean! Why will you not ask me to dine with, him en famille?

> {Yes.}
> {A.D.}

* * * * *

EMMA TO NELSON.

  I think, I have not lost my heart;
    Since I, with truth, can swear,
  At every moment of my life,
    I feel my Nelson there!

  If, from thine Emma's breast, her heart
    Were stolen or flown away;
  Where! where! should she my Nelson's love
    Record, each happy day?

  If, from thine Emma's breast, her heart
    Were stolen or flown away;
  Where! where! should she engrave, my Love!
    Each tender word you say?

  Where! where! should Emma treasure up
    Her Nelson's smiles and sighs?

Where mark, with joy, each secret look
  Of love, from Nelson's eyes?

Then, do not rob me of my heart,
  Unless you first forsake it;
And, then, so wretched it would be,
  Despair alone will take it.

Letter from Lady Hamilton TO THE RIGHT HONOURABLE HENRY ADDINGTON, NOW VISCOUNT SIDMOUTH.

Letter of Lady Hamilton, &c.

April 13th. [1803.]

SIR,

May I trouble you, and but for a moment, in consequence of my irreparable loss; my ever-honoured husband, Sir William Hamilton, being no more! I cannot avoid it, I am forced to petition for a portion of his pension: such a portion as, in your wisdom and noble nature, may be approved; and so represented to our most gracious Sovereign, as being right. For, Sir, I am most sadly bereaved! I am now in circumstances far below those in which the goodness of my dear Sir William allowed me to move for so many years; and below those becoming the relict of such a public minister, who was proved so very long—no less than thirty-six years—and, all his life, honoured so very much by the constant friendly kindness of the King and Queen themselves: and, may I mention—what is well known to the then administration at home—how I, too, strove to do all I could towards the service of our King and Country. The fleet itself, I can truly say, could not have got into Sicily, but for what I was happily able to do with the Queen of Naples, and through her secret instructions so obtained: on which depended the refitting of the fleet in Sicily; and, with that, all which followed so gloriously at the Nile. These few words, though seemingly much at large, may not be extravagant at all. They are, indeed, true.

I wish them to be heard, only as they can be proved; and, being proved, may I hope for what I have now desired?

I am, Sir, with respect more than I can well utter, your obedient servant,

EMMA HAMILTON.

Letters FROM SIR WILLIAM HAMILTON, K.B. TO LADY HAMILTON.

Letters OF SIR WILLIAM HAMILTON, K.B. &c.

I.

Persano, [Wednesday]
Jan. 4, 1792.

We arrived here, yesterday, in little more than five hours, and had nearly began with a disagreeable accident; for the King's horse took fright at the guard, and his Majesty and horse were as near down as possible. However, all ended well; and he was as gay as possible, yesterday.

Our first chasse has not succeeded; though there were two wolves, and many wild boars, in the Mena: but the king would direct how we should beat the wood, and began at the wrong end; by which the wolves and boars escaped, and we remained without shooting power. However, ten or twelve boars have been killed, some how or other, and some large ones.

The King's face is very long, at this moment; but, I dare say, to-morrow's good sport will shorten it again.

I was sorry, my dear Em. to leave you in affliction: you must harden yourself to such little misfortunes as a temporary parting; but, I cannot blame you for having a good and tender heart. Believe me, you are in thorough possession of all mine, though I will allow it to be rather tough.

Let us study to make one another as comfortable as we can; and "banish sorrow, till to-morrow:" and so on, every day.

You are wise enough to see the line it is proper for you to take; and have, hitherto, followed it most rigorously: and I can assure you, that I have not the least doubt of your continuing in it.

Amuse yourself as well as you can, as I am doing, whilst we are separate; and the best news you can give me is, that you are well and happy.

My cold is already better for having passed the whole day in the open air, and without human seccatura.

Adieu! my dear, dear Emma. I am, with my love to your good mother, your's ever, and faithfully,

W.H.

II.

Persano, Thursday,
[Jan. 5th, 1792.]

We got home early, and I have not yet received your Daily Advertiser.

No sport, again! In the midst of such a quantity of game, they have contrived to carry him far off, where there is none. He has no other comfort, to-day, than having killed a wild cat; and his face is a yard long.

However, his Majesty has vowed vengeance on the boars to-morrow, and will go according to his own fancy; and, I dare say, there will be a terrible slaughter.

The last day, we are to keep all we kill; and, I suppose, it will be night before we get home.

Yesterday, the courier brought the order of St. Stephano, from the Emperor, for the Prince Ausberg, and the King was desired to invest him with it. As soon as the King received it, he ran into the Prince's room; whom he found in his shirt, and without his breeches: and, in that condition, was he decorated with the star and ribbon by his Majesty, who has wrote the whole circumstance to the Emperor.

Leopold may, perhaps, not like the joking with his first order. Such nonsense should, certainly, be done with solemnity; or it becomes, what it really is, a little tinsel, and a few yards of broad ribbon.

The Prince, entre nous, is not very wise; but he is a good creature and we are great friends.

I have wrote to Mrs. Dickinson. I forget whether you have, or not: if not, pray do it soon; for, you know, she is a good friend of your's.

I have just received your good letter. I am glad they have taken the Guarda patana's son-in-law. I insist upon Smith's letting the Regent of the Vicaria know of his having stabbed my porter. He ought to go to the gallies; and my honour is concerned, if this insult offered my livery is unnoticed. The girl had better cry, than be ill-used, and her father killed.

Adieu, my sweet Em. Your's, with all my heart,

W.H.

III.

Persano, Friday Evening.
[Jan. 6th, 1792.]

I Inclose our friend Knight's admirable letter to you. I could not refrain reading it; and, I am sure, it was his intention I should do so, having left it unsealed. He is a fine fellow; it was worth going to England, to secure such a sensible friend.

You will probably have seen General Werner last night; this is Friday night, and he will have told you I am well.

We have been out all day in the rain; I killed none, and the King and party but few. Such obstinate bad weather I really never experienced, for so long a time together.

You did perfectly right in buying the lamps; and I am glad the Prince asked to dine with you. I am sure, he was comfortably received by you.

You see what devils [there are] in England! They wanted to stir up something against me; but our conduct shall be such as to be unattackable: and I fear not an injustice from England. Twenty-seven years service—having spent all the King's money, and all my own, besides running in debt, deserves something better than a dismission!

The King has declared, he will return to Naples next Saturday se'n-night; so you know the worst, my dear Emma. Indeed, I shall embrace you most cordially; for I would not be married to any woman, but yourself, on earth, for all the world.

Lord A. Hamilton's son, you see, recommends a friend of his; who, I suppose, is arrived: if so, receive him well.

Adieu, again! Your's, ever,

W.H.

IV.

Persano, Saturday Night,
[January 7th, 1792.]

This has been one of the cruel days which attend the King's chasse. All the posts—except the King's, Prince Ausberg, D'Onerato, and Priori—bad.

We have been out all day, in cold rain, without seeing a boar. The King has killed twenty-five, and a wolf; and the other good posts, in proportion.

Why not rather leave us at home, than go out with the impossibility of sport? But we must take the good and bad, or give it up.

Lamberg is too delicate for this business; he has been in bed, with a slight fever, all to-day.

You will have another boar, to-day; which boar being a sow, I have made a bull! The sows are much better than the boars; so you may keep some to eat at home, and dispose of the rest to your favourite English.

I am glad all goes on so well. I never doubted your gaining every soul you approach.

I am far from being angry at your feeling the loss of me so much! Nay, I am flattered; but, believe me, the time will soon come, that we shall meet. Years pass seemingly in an instant; why, then, afraid of a few days?

Upon the whole, we are sociable here; but we go to bed at nine, and get up at five o'clock. I generally read an hour, to digest my supper; but, indeed, I live chiefly on bread and butter.

Salandra desires his compliments to you, as does Lamberg and Prince Ausberg.

Adieu, my dear Emma! Ever your's, and your's alone,

  W.H.

I send you back your two letters. Dutens was very satisfactory. I send the papers to Smith; who will give them to you first, if you have not read them.

The cold and fatigue makes my hand something like your's—which, by the bye, you neglect rather too much: but, as what you write is good sense, every body will forgive the scrawl.

V.

Sunday Night, [Jan. 8th, 1792.]

We are come in late; and I have but a moment to tell you we are well, and I have killed three large boars, a fox, and four woodcocks.

Nothing pleases me more, than to hear you do not neglect your singing.
 It would be a pity, as you are near the point of perfection.

Adieu, my dearest Emma! Your's, with my whole soul,

W.H.

VI.

Persano, [Monday]
January 10th, [9th] 1792.

Your letter of yesterday, my Sweet Em. gave me great pleasure; as, I see, all goes on perfectly right for you at Naples.

Your business, and mine, is to be civil to all, and not enter into any party matters. If the Wilkinsons are not content with our civilities, let them help themselves.

We have had a charming day, and most excellent sport. More than a hundred wild boars, and two wolves, have fallen. I killed five boars, truly monsters! and a fox.

Vincenzo could not follow me to-day; he cannot walk two steps, without being out of breath. However, I load the guns myself; and, with the peasant I brought from Caserta, and another I hire here, I do very well. I fear, poor Vincenzo will not hold long. If he chooses it, I mean to send him to Naples, to consult Noody [Nudi.]

General Werner, Prince of Hesse, and Count Zichare, are here since last night; they brought me your compliments. Lamberg is still confined.

Amuse yourself, my dearest Emma, and never doubt of my love. Your's, ever,

W.H.

VII.

Persano, [Tuesday]
Jan. 10th, 1792.

The day has been so thoroughly bad, that we have not been able to stir out; and the King, of course, in bad humour. I am not sorry to have a day's repose, and I have wrote my letters for to-morrow's post.

Lamberg is still in bed with a fever, and Prince Ausberg's eyes are a little inflamed with cold and fatigue. My cold was renewed a little yesterday; but a good night's rest, and quiet to-day, has set all to rights again.

Vincenzo was so bad, yesterday, that he could not follow me, and was blooded. He is better, to-day; but he will never serve more, except to load my guns at the post. He cannot walk a mile, without being out of breath.

I am glad you have been at the Academy, and in the great world. It is time enough for you to find out, that the only real comfort is to be met with at home; I have been in that secret some time.

You are, certainly, the most domestic young woman I know: but you are young, and most beautiful; and it would not be natural, if you did not like to shew yourself a little in public.

The effusion of tenderness, with regard to me, in your letter, is very flattering; I know the value of it, and will do all I can to keep it alive. We are now one flesh, and it must be our study to keep that flesh as warm and comfortable as we can. I will do all in my power to please you, and I do not doubt of your doing the same towards me.

Adieu, my dearest Emma! Having nothing interesting to write, and as you insist upon hearing from me every day, you must content yourself with such a stupid letter as this.

Your Ladyship's commands shall always be punctually obeyed by, dear
 Madam, your Ladyship's most obedient and faithful servant,

W. HAMILTON.

VIII.

Persano, Wednesday,
11th Jan. [1792.]

I have just received your letter—and, as I always do—with infinite pleasure.

I hope you received twelve wood-biddies, to-day; and, to-morrow, you will have a wild boar: all left to your discretion.

No talk of returning, yet. We must complete sixteen days shooting, and one day has been lost by bad weather.

We had a good day, and tolerable sport. I have killed two, and one the largest boar I have seen yet here.

Vincenzo, they say, will be well in a day or two, as it is only a cold; I fear, it is more serious.

The King has killed twenty-one boars to-day, and is quite happy.

The Germans all drink tea with me every evening. Lamberg is better.

Adieu, my ever dear Emma! We are always in a hurry; though we have, absolutely, nothing to do, but kill, examine, and weigh, wild boars.

I assure you, that I shall rejoice when I can embrace you once more. A picture would not content me; your image is more strongly represented on my heart, than any that could be produced by human art.

Your most affectionate husband,

W.H.

IX.

Persano, Thursday Night,
[Jan. 12th, 1792.]

Never put yourself in a hurry, my dear Emma.

I have got your two kind letters. Send for Gasparo; and give your orders, that the servants attend your call: and let him discharge them, if they do not. You are my better half, and may command. Translate this part of the letter to him.

We have had good sport to-day, though the bad weather came on at eleven o'clock. Fifty-four wild boars have been killed, I had seven shot; and killed five, three of which are enormous. Dispose of the boar I send you to-day as you think proper.

I always thought Ruspoli a dirty fellow; but what has he done of late?

As to your mother's going with you to the English parties, very well; but, believe me, it will be best for her, and more to her happiness, to stay at home, than go with you to the Neapolitan parties.

The King is in good humour to-day, as I foretold. We continue to dine at eight at night, and have nothing from breakfast to that hour. But I give tea and bread and butter, of which Prince Ausberg and Lamberg partake with pleasure. The Prince, having no opportunity of making love, does nothing but talk of his new flame, which is Lady A. Hatton. I put him right; for he thought she spelt her name with two rr, instead of two tt.

I rejoice at your having Aprile again; pray, tell him so: for I know the rapid progress you will make under his care.

My cold is near gone. The worst is, my room smokes confoundedly; and so do all the other rooms, except the King's.

Adieu, my dear Emma! Amuse yourself as well as you can; and believe me, ever, your's alone, with the utmost confidence,

W.H.

X.

Persano, Friday Night,
 [Jan. 13th, 1792.]

We have had a miserable cold day, but good sport. I killed two boars, and a doe; the King, nineteen boars, two stags, two does, and a porcupine. He is happy beyond expression.

I send you Charles's letter; but do not lose it, as I will answer it when I return. You see, the line we have taken will put it out of the power of our enemies to hurt us. I will give up my judgment of worldly matters to no one.

I approve of all you do in my absence; but it would be nonsense, and appear affected, to carry your scruples too far. Divert yourself reasonably. I am sure of your attachment to me, and I shall not easily be made to alter my opinion of you.

My cold is better, notwithstanding the weather.

I have no time to in'gler; so, adieu! my dearest wife.

Your's,

W.H.

P.S. Let Gasparo pay thirty ducats, for the vase, to D. Andrea.

By way of charity, we may give thirty ounces to that shabby dog, Hadrava; though he knows the picture is not worth more than ten at most. His writing to you in such a stile is pitiful indeed. You will often have such letters, if you do not tell him, now, that it is for once and all.

XI.

Persano, Saturday, 14th Jan. [1792.]

MY DEAR EMMA,

I have received a letter from Douglass; with one inclosed, from Mr. Durno; who, to my surprise, says, he has not received my order on Biddulph, Cockes, and Co. for one thousand five hundred and ninety pounds; which, you know, I sent from Caserta.

I find, in my book of letters, 20th of December, that I wrote, that day, a letter to Mr. Burgess, to deliver to Messieurs Biddulph and Co.—to Lord Abercorn—and to Mr. Durno, with the order inclosed.

Pray, send for Smith; and ask him, if he remembers having put such letters in the post, and let him inquire at the Naples post about them: and let him send the inclosed, by Tuesday's post, to Rome.

I certainly will not give another order until this matter is cleared up. I fear some roguery.

We have had a fine day, and killed numberless boars; a hundred and fifty, at least. I have killed four, out of six shot; and am satisfied, as one is a real monster—the King, thirty—D'Onerato, eighteen,—and so on, the favoured shooters.

Vincenzo is rather better, but not able to serve me.

My best compliments to Alexander Hamilton. You did well, to invite
 Copley.

Adieu! my sweet Em. Ever your's, in deed and in truth,

W.H.

XII.

Persano, Sunday,
Jan. 15, 1792.

You did admirably, my Dear Em. in not inviting Lady A.H. to dine with the Prince; and still better, in telling her, honestly, the reason. I have always found, that going straight is the best method, though not the way of the world.

You did, also, very well, in asking Madame Skamouski; and not taking upon you to present her, without leave.

In short, consult your own good sense, and do not be in a hurry; and, I am sure, you will always act right.

We have been at it again, this morning, and killed fifty boars; but were home to dinner, at one o'clock: and this is the first dinner I have had, since I left you; for I cannot eat meat breakfasts or suppers, and have absolutely lived on bread and butter and tea.

As the Prince asked you, you did well to send for a song to Douglass's; but, in general, you will do right to sing only at home.

The King is very kind to me, and shews every one that he really loves me: and he commends my shooting; having missed but very few, and killed the largest of the society. Only think of his not being satisfied with killing more than thirty, yesterday! He said, if the wind had favoured him, he should have killed sixty at least.

We must be civil to Mr. Hope, as recommended by Lord Auckland; and also to Monsieur de Rochement, and Prince Bozatinsky, as recommended by my friend Saussure. I inclose his letter, as you are mentioned in it; also Knight's, as you desire. God knows, we have no secrets; nor, I hope, ever shall.

We have much business between this and Saturday: and we are to shoot, Saturday morning; so that we shall arrive late.

What say you to a feet washing that night? O che Gusto! when your prima ora is over, and all gone.

Adieu, my sweet Emma! Ever your's,

W.H.

XIII.

Persano, Monday Night,
 [Jan. 16th, 1792.]

For your long and interesting letter, I can only write a line, to tell you I am well.

We have been out, till an hour in the night, from day-break; and I have fired off my gun but once, having had a bad post. The King, and favoured party, have diverted themselves. To-morrow will, probably, be a good day for me.

Pray, let Smith get orders for the Museum, &c. for Lord Boyle and Mr. Dodge, as they are recommended by Mr. Eden.

Adieu, my lovely Emma! Let them all roll on the carpet, &c. provided you are not of the party. My trust is in you alone.

Your's, ever,

W.H.

XIV.

Persano, Tuesday Night,
[Jan. 17, 1792.]

I told you, my Dear Em. that I expected good sport to-day! I have killed five boars, and two great ones got off after falling; two bucks; six does; and a hare: fourteen in all.

By the bye, I must tell you, that accept and except are totally different. You always write—"I did not except of the invitation;" when, you know, it should be "accept." It is, only, for want of giving yourself time to think; but, as this error has been repeated, I thought best to tell you of it.

Pray, write a very kind letter to our friend the Archbishop; and convince him, that Emma, to her friends, is unalterable. Do not say a word about the telescope; for, I must try it, first, against mine. If it should be better, I cannot part with it, as you know how much use we make of a telescope.

The King has killed eighty-one animals, of one sort or other, to-day; and, amongst them, a wolf, and some stags. He fell asleep in the coach; and, waking, told me he had been dreaming of shooting. One would have thought, he had shed blood enough.

This is a heavy air; nobody eats with appetite, and many are ill with colds.

We shall be home on Saturday; and, indeed, my sweet Emma, I shall be most happy to see you.

To-morrow, we go to a mountain; but no great expectation of sport.

Your's, ever, my dear wife,

 W.H.

XV.

Persano, Wednesday,
[Jan. 18th, 1792.]

It was not your white and silver, alone, that made you look like an angel, at the Academy. Suppose you had put it on nine parts out of ten of the ladies in company, would any one have appeared angelic?

I will allow, however, that a beautiful woman, feeling herself well dressed, will have a sort of confidence, which will add greatly to the lustre of her eye: but take my word, that, for some years to come, the more simply you dress, the more conspicuous will be your beauty; which, according to my idea, is the most perfect I have yet met with, take it all in all.

It is long-faced day with the King. We went far; the weather was bad; and, after all, met with little or no game: I did not fire off my gun.

Yesterday, when we brought home all we killed, it filled the house, completely; and, to-day, they are obliged to white-wash the walls, to take away the blood. There were more than four hundred; boars, deer, stags, and all.

To-morrow, we are to have another slaughter; and not a word of reason or common sense do I meet with, the whole day, till I retire to my volumes of the old Gentleman's Magazine, which just keeps my mind from starving.

Except to-day, on a mountain, I have never felt the least appetite; there, I eat the wings of a cold chicken with pleasure.

Hamilton is delighted with your civilities. He has wrote me a long letter. I do not mean to keep pace with him in writing; so, send him a line or two, only, in answer.

I do not recollect the name of Marino Soolania; and, if I received a letter from him, it was in the hurry of my arrival, and is lost: so that Smith may desire the Dutch Consul to desire him to write again, and I will answer.

I always rejoice when I find you do not neglect your singing. I am, I own, ambitious of producing something extraordinary in you, and it is nearly done.

Adieu! my sweet Em. I rejoice that the time of our re-union is so near—Saturday night!

W.H.

XVI.

Venasso, Friday, 27th January 1794.

MY DEAR EM.

By having grumbled a little, I got a better post to-day; and have killed two boars and a sow, all enormous. I have missed but two shot since I came here; and, to be sure, when the post is good, it is noble shooting! The rocks, and mountains, as wild as the boars.

The news you sent me, of poor Lord Pembroke, gave me a little twist; but I have, for some time, perceived, that my friends, with whom I spent my younger days, have been dropping around me.

Lord Pembroke's neck was very short, and his father died of an apoplexy.

My study of antiquities, has kept me in constant thought of the perpetual fluctuation of everything. The whole art is, really, to live all the days of our life; and not, with anxious care, disturb the sweetest hour that life affords—which is, the present! Admire the Creator, and all his works, to us incomprehensible: and do all the good you can upon earth; and take the chance of eternity, without dismay.

You must tell the Archbishop, that he will have the Leyden gazettes a week later; as I cannot read them time enough to send by this messenger.

The weather is delightful; and, I believe, we shall have done all our business, so as to return on Thursday.

Pray, find out if the Queen goes to Caserta. Here, all is a profound secret.

I must work hard, myself, at translating, when I return; for I believe the language-master totally incapable of it.

I dined, this morning, at nine o'clock; and, I think, it agreed better with me than tea. I found myself growing weak, for want of a good meal, not daring to eat much at supper.

Adieu, my sweet love! adieu. Divert yourself—I shall soon be at you again. Your's, ever,

W.H.

XVII.

Burford, Eighty Miles from London.
Saturday Night, [July 27th, 1801.]

Here we are, my Dear Emma, after a pleasant day's journey! No extraordinary occurrence. Our chaise is good, and would have held the famous "Tria juncta in Uno," very well: but, we must submit to the circumstances of the times.

Sir Joseph Bankes we found in bed with the gout: and, last night, his hot-house was robbed of its choicest fruit—peaches and nectarines.

Amuse yourself as well as you can; and you may be assured, that I shall return as soon as possible, and you shall hear from me often.

Ever your's, my dear Emma, with the truest affection,

Wm. HAMILTON.

My kindest love to my Lord, if he is not gone.

P.S. Corn, at this market, fell fifteen pounds a load to-day.

Letters FROM SIR WILLIAM HAMILTON, K.B. TO LORD NELSON.

Letters OF SIR WILLIAM HAMILTON, K.B. &c.

I.

[Written before LORD NELSON'S Elevation to the Peerage.]

Naples, March 26th, 1796.

MY DEAR SIR,

The moment I received your letter of the 11th of March from Leghorn, I went with it to General Acton: and, although I could not, from your letter only, in my Ministerial character, demand from this Court the assistance of some of their xebecs, corvettes, &c. that are the fittest for going near shore; as I think, with you, that such vessels are absolutely necessary on the present occasion, I told his Excellency—that I trusted, as this government had hitherto shewn itself as sanguine in the good cause, and more so, than any of the allies of Great Britain, that he would lay your letter before the King at Naples; and, without waiting for the demand which I should probably receive soon from Sir John Jervis, send you such small armed vessels as his Excellency thought would be proper for the service on which you are employed.

The General, without hesitation, said—that orders should be immediately given for the preparing of such a flotilla, which should join you as soon as the weather would permit. At present, indeed, it is not very encouraging for row-boats.

We wait a courier from Vienna, to decide the march of eight thousand eight hundred infantry, and artillery included, intended to join the Emperor's army in Italy: and, although the Grand Duke of Tuscany has refused the permission for these troops to march through his dominions, the King of Naples has told his son-in-law that, whenever the safety of Italy should require it, he would, nevertheless, march them through Tuscany; a liberty which the Emperor would likewise take, whenever the good of the service required it.

However, the thousand cavalry sent from hence have taken their route, by Loretto, through the Pope's state.

We have had, as I suppose you know, the Admirals Hotham and Goodall here, for some weeks. I can, entre nous, perceive that my old friend Hotham is not quite awake enough for such a command as that of the King's fleet in the Mediterranean, although he appears the best creature imaginable.

I did not know much of your friend Lord Hood, personally; but, by his correspondence with me, his activity and clearness was most conspicuous.

Lady Hamilton and I admire your constancy, and hope the severe service you have undergone will be handsomely rewarded.

When I reported to Lord Grenville, in my last dispatch, the letter I received from you lately, I could not help giving you the epithet of "that brave officer, Captain Nelson." If you do not deserve it, I know not who does.

With our love to Sam, I am, ever, dear Sir, your's, sincerely,

Wm. HAMILTON.

II.

Palermo, February 13th, 1799.

MY LORD,

Having received an application from this government, that they might be supplied with lead from on board the British merchants ships in this harbour, that have that article on board—and that, without the help of about a hundred cantarra of lead, this country, and the common cause, would be much distressed—I am to beg of your Lordship to use your kind endeavours that this urgent want may be supplied as soon as possible: well understood, that the proprietors of this article should be perfectly satisfied with this government, as to the price of the lead, freight, &c.

I have the honour to be, my Lord, your Lordship's most obedient and most humble servant,

Wm. HAMILTON.

III.

Palermo, Sunday Night late, near winding-up-watch hour, May 19th, 1799.

MY VERY DEAR LORD,

Ten thousand thanks for your kind attention in sending us Hallowell's letter to Troubridge. It comforts us in one respect, as it flatters us with Commodore Duckworth's four ships joining you soon. But, I must own, from the junction of five Spanish ships and frigates, I now think, something more than going into Toulon is intended, and that your Lordship may have a brush with them.

God send you every success, that your unparalleled virtues and bravery so well merit.

Adieu, my dear Lord! Your Lordship's truly affectionate, and eternally attached,

Wm. HAMILTON.

IV.

Palermo, May 26th, 1799.

MY DEAR LORD,

Whilst Emma was writing to your Lordship, I have been with Acton, to get a felucca, to send Ball's dispatch to you. It is of so old a date, that I make no doubt of Ball's having joined you before his dispatch reaches.

I send your Lordship an interesting letter I have just received from our Consul at Trieste: and Acton's answer to my yesterday's letter communicating your kind resolution of taking care of their Sicilian Majesties and their kingdoms; and which, your Lordship will see, gives them great satisfaction.

As to the fleet having been seen by the Towers near Messina, and to the westward—I believe, it was your squadron.

I send you, likewise, a strange rhapsody from Lord Bristol: but something may be collected from it; or, at least, it will amuse you, and you have leisure enough on board, which I have not on shore. Be so good as to send back that letter, and Graham's, by the first opportunity.

Above all, take care of your health; that is the first of blessings. May God ever protect you! We miss you heavily: but, a short time must clear up the business; and, we hope, bring you back to those who love and esteem you to the very bottom of their souls.

Ever your affectionate friend, and humble servant,

Wm. HAMILTON.

V.

Palermo, June 17th, 1799.

MY DEAR LORD,

I am happy to receive the packet from Major Magra, and which I shall instantly send to General Acton.

Nothing has happened, worth telling you, since the few hours we have been separated.

God bless you, my very dear friend; and my mind tells me, that you will soon have reason, either by good news, or by a proper reinforcement sent to you, to be in a much happier state of mind than you could possibly be when you left us this morning. All looks melancholy without you.

Ever, my dear Lord, your truly attached friend,

Wm. HAMILTON.

VI.

Palermo, June 20th, 1799.
Eight o'Clock at Night.

MY DEAR LORD,

Having wrote fully by the felucca to-day, that went off at three o'clock—and have not yet General Acton's answer, with respect to what the Court would wish you to do when you hear how the French fleet is disposed of—I have nothing to write by the transport.

God bless you! And I hope, somehow or other, we shall meet again soon.

My dear Lord, your's, most sincerely,

Wm. HAMILTON.

VII.

Piccadilly, February 19th, 1801.

MY DEAR LORD,

Whether Emma will be able to write to you to-day, or not, is a question; as she has got one of her terrible sick head-achs. Among other things that vex her, is—that we have been drawn in to be under the absolute necessity of giving a dinner to ****** on Sunday next. He asked it himself; having expressed his strong desire of hearing Banti's and Emma's voices together.

I am well aware of the danger that would attend ******* frequenting our house. Not that I fear, that Emma could ever be induced to act contrary to the prudent conduct she has hitherto pursued; but the world is so ill-natured, that the worst construction is put upon the most innocent actions.

As this dinner must be, or ****** would be offended, I shall keep it strictly to the musical part; invite only Banti, her husband, and Taylor; and, as I wish to shew a civility to Davison, I have sent him an invitation.

In short, we will get rid of it as well as we can, and guard against its producing more meetings of the same sort.

Emma would really have gone any lengths, to have avoided Sunday's dinner. But I thought it would not be prudent to break with ******; who, really, has shewn the greatest civility to us, when we were last in England, and since we returned: and she has, at last, acquiesced to my opinion.

I have been thus explicit, as I know well your Lordship's way of thinking; and your very kind attachment to us, and to every thing that concerns us.

The King caught cold at the Chapel the other day, and there was no levee yesterday; and, to-day, the Queen alone will be at the drawing-room: and, I believe, the new ministry will not be quite fixed, until the levee-day next week.

As to my business—I have done all I can to bring it to a point.

The pension recommended by Lord Grenville was only like Walpole's—a nominal two thousand pounds. I have represented the injustice of that—after my having had the King's promise of not being removed from Naples, but at my own request; and having only empowered Lord Grenville to remove me, on securing to me a nett income of two thousand pounds per annum.

Lord Grenville has recommended to the Treasury, the taking my extraordinary expences into consideration.

I have fully demonstrated, to Lord Grenville and Treasury, that eight thousand pounds is absolutely necessary for the clearing off my unfunded debt, without making up for my losses.

Upon the whole, then, I do not expect to get more than the nett annuity above mentioned, and the eight thousand pounds. But, unless that is granted, I shall, indeed, have been very ill-used! I hope, in my next, to be able to inform your Lordship that all has been finally settled.

I am busy in putting in order the remains of my vases and pictures, that you so kindly saved for me on board the

Fourdroyant; and the sale of them will enable me to go on more at my ease, and not leave a debt unpaid. But, unfortunately, there have been too many picture sales this year, and mine will come late.

Adieu! my very dear Lord. May health and success attend you, wherever you go! And, I flatter myself, this political jumble may hasten a peace, and bring you back soon.

Your Lordship's ever obliged, and most sincerely attached, friend and servant,

Wm. HAMILTON.

VIII.

Piccadilly, February 20th, 1801.

MY DEAR LORD,

You need not be the least alarmed, that Emma has commissioned me to send you the newspapers; and write you a line, to tell you that she is much better—having vomited naturally, and is now purposing to take a regular one of tartar emetic.

All her convulsive complaints certainly proceed from a foul stomach; and I will answer for it, she will be in spirits to write to you herself to-morrow.

Adieu! my very dear Lord. I have not a moment to lose, as the bell is going.

Your ever attached and obliged humble servant,

Wm. HAMILTON.

IX.

Piccadilly, March 7th, 1801.

MY VERY DEAR LORD,

I wish it was in my power to profit of your kind invitation; you would soon see me and Emma on board the St. George: but I am now totally occupied in preparing for the sale of my pictures, and what I have saved of my vases.

To my great satisfaction, I have found some of the most capital vases; and which I thought, surely, lost on board the Colossus. It has comforted me much.

We remain in the same cruel state with respect to the King's recovery. There can be no doubt, but that his Majesty is better. However, if my conjectures are true, the Regency must soon take place: as it may be long before his Majesty could be troubled with business, supposing even his fever to have totally subsided; and, the times admit of no delays.

We see, now, the certainty of the French squadron's being in the Mediterranean. God knows, how all this will end! But I hope it will be your Lordship's lot to bring Paul to his senses.

God send you every success; and send you home, safe and well, crowned with additional laurels! And then, I hope, you will repose your shattered frame; and make your friends happy, by staying with them.

Emma

Emma is certainly much better, but not quite free from bile.

Ever, my dear Lord, your Lordship's most attached, and eternally obliged, humble servant,

Wm. HAMILTON.

X.

Piccadilly, April 16th, 1801.

What can I say, my Dear Lord! that would convey the smallest idea of what we felt yesterday, on receiving the authentic letters confirming your late most glorious victory: and read, in your own hand, that God had not only granted you complete success against the enemies of our country; but, in the midst of such perils, prevented your receiving the smallest scratch!

We can only repeat what we knew well, and often said, before—that Nelson was, is, and to the last will ever be, the first.

However, we all agree that, when we get you safe home once more—that you should never more risk your shattered frame.

You have done enough, and are well entitled to the motto of Virgil—

"Hic Victor cæstus artemque repono."

The famous Broughton, after he had beaten every opponent, that dared to measure hard blows with him, set up an ale-house—the Broughton's Head—in London, with the above verse of Virgil under it. Some years after, he was persuaded to accept the challenge of a coachman, and was beaten.

Not that I mean to convey, that any such thing could happen to your Lordship; but, you have done enough. Let others follow your examples; they will be remembered to the latest posterity.

It appeared to me most extraordinary, that the 6th inst. the date of your last letter to Emma, the death of the Emperor Paul (which we have no doubt of here) should not be known at Copenhagen!

It appears to us that, as soon as that great event is known in Sweden and Denmark, with the severe blow you have just given the latter, the formidable giant, Northern Coalition, will of itself fall to pieces; and that we shall have the happiness of embracing you again here, in a very short time.

You would have laughed to have seen what I saw yesterday! Emma did not know whether she was on her head or heels—in such a hurry to tell your great news, that she could utter nothing but tears of joy and tenderness.

I went to Davison yesterday morning; and found him still in bed, having had a severe fit of the gout, and with your letter, which he had just received: and he cried like a child! But, what was very extraordinary, assured me that, from the instant he had read your letter, all pain had left him, and that he felt himself able to get up and walk about.

Your brother, Mrs. Nelson, and Horace, dined with us. Your brother was more extraordinary than ever. He would get up suddenly, and cut a caper; rubbing his hands every time that the thought of your fresh laurels came into his head.

In short, except myself, (and your Lordship knows that I have some phlegm) all the company, which was considerable, after dinner—the Duke, Lord William, Mr. Este, &c.—were mad with joy. But, I am sure, that no one really rejoiced more, at heart, than I did. I have lived too long to have extacies! But, with calm reflection, I felt for my friend having got to the very summit of glory!—the "Ne plus ultra!"—that he has had another opportunity of rendering his country the most important service; and manifesting, again, his judgment, his intrepidity, and humanity.

God bless you, my very dear Lord, and send you soon home to your friends. Enemies you have none, but those that are bursting with envy; and such animals infest all parts of the world.

The King, be assured, is (though weak) getting well fast. Lord Loughborough told Livingston, who has just been here, that he was with the King the day before yesterday, before and after delivery of the seals, and that he was perfectly calm and recollected.

Ever your sincerely attached, and truly obliged, humble servant,

Wm. HAMILTON.

XI.

Milford, August 12th, 1801.

MY DEAR LORD,

Emma has constantly given me every possible intelligence relative to your Lordship, and the important operations you are about at this most interesting moment.

You have already calmed the minds of every body with respect to the threatened French invasion. In short, all your Lordship does is complete; like yourself, and nobody else. But still, I think, there is no occasion for the Commander in Chief to expose his person as much as you do. Why should you not have a private flag, known to your fleet and not to the enemy, when you shift it and go reconnoitring?

Captain Hopkins, going from hence in the Speedwell cutter to join your Lordship, will be happy to introduce himself to you by presenting this letter himself. They give him a good character in this country, but my acquaintance with him is but of two days.

I was yesterday with Captain Dobbins, in the Diligence cutter. We sailed out of this glorious harbour; and, the day being fine, sailed out some leagues, and examined the Crow Rock, which is reckoned the greatest danger as to entering the harbour. But the two light-houses lately erected take off all danger in the night; and [it] is visible in the day-time, except a short time in spring tides.

I am delighted with the improvements at Milford. It will surely be a great town, if we have peace, in three years; the houses rising up, like mushrooms, even in these difficult times. We allow any one to build—at their own expence—

at an easy ground-rent, and to fall in at the expiration of three lives, or sixty years.

You may judge that, having two thousand acres all round the town, these inhabitants will want land for cows and horses, and gardens, &c. and, of course, I must be a gainer in the end.

I visited the two light-houses, and found them perfectly clean, and in good order: and I never could conceive the brilliant light that they give; one has sixteen reflected lights, and the other ten.

To-day, I go upon my last visit to Lord Milford; and, on Saturday, set out for Piccadilly: and where I am not without hopes of meeting your Lordship; as I think, in the manner you dispatch business, you will have completed all by Wednesday next, the day I shall probably be in London.

Charles Greville's kind compliments. The name of Nelson is in every mouth; and, indeed, we owe every thing to your judgment and exertions.

Adieu! God bless you. Ever your Lordship's affectionate friend, and obliged humble servant,

Wm. HAMILTON.

XII.

Piccadilly, April 28th, 1802.

MY DEAR LORD,

Emma says—I must write a letter to you, of condolence for the heavy loss your Lordship has suffered.

When persons, in the prime of life, are carried off by accidents or sickness—or what is, I believe, oftener the case, by the ignorance and mistakes of the physicians—then, indeed, there is reason to lament! But as, in the case of your good Father, the lamp was suffered to burn out fairly, and that his sufferings were not great; and that, by his Son's glorious and unparalleled successes, he saw his family ennobled, and with the probability, in time, of its being amply rewarded, as it ought to have been long ago—his mind could not be troubled, in his latter moments, on account of the family he left behind him: and, as to his own peace of mind, at the moment of his dissolution, there can be no doubt, among those who ever had the honour of his acquaintance.

I have said more than I intended; but dare say, your Lordship had nearly the same thoughts—with the addition of the feelings of a dutiful Son, for the loss of a most excellent Father.

It is, however, now—as your Lordship is the Father of your Family—incumbent upon you to take particular care of your own health.
Nay, you are, by the voice of the nation, its first prop and support.

Keep up your spirits; and, that you may long enjoy your well-earned honours, is the sincere wish of your Lordship's affectionate friend, and attached humble servant,

Wm. HAMILTON.

Letters FROM LORD NELSON TO SIR WILLIAM HAMILTON, K.B.

Letters OF LORD NELSON, &c.

I.

Bastia, May 24th, 1794.

MY DEAR SIR,

Will you have the goodness to forward the inclosed to Mr. Brand, and to present my letter to Lady Hamilton?

Every lover of his country will rejoice in our great and almost unexampled success, to the honour of my Lord Hood, and to the shame of those who opposed his endeavours to serve his country.

General Stewart, I am happy to say, is just arrived.

We shall now join, heart and hand, against Calvi. When conquered, I shall hope to pay my respects to your Excellency at Naples; which will give real pleasure to your very faithful, and obliged,

HORATIO NELSON.

II.

Agamemnon, Leghorn,
  March 11th, 1796.

SIR,

Mr. Wyndham having communicated to Mr. Udney the conversation of the French minister with the Tuscans, I cannot, being intrusted by the Admiral with the command of the small squadron in the Gulph of Genoa, but think it right for me to beg that your Excellency will apply for such vessels of war belonging to his Sicilian Majesty, as may be judged proper to cruize in the Gulph of Genoa, and particularly off the point of the Gulph of Especia. Xebecs, corvettes, and frigates, are the fittest to cruize; and the first have the great advantage of rowing, as well as sailing, I am told, very fast.

General [Acton] knows, full as well as myself, the vessels proper to prevent the disembarkation of troops on this coast; therefore, I shall not particularly point them out.

Last campaign, the word flotilla was misunderstood. I can only say, that all vessels which can sail and row must be useful; and, for small craft, Port Especia is a secure harbour.

Whatever is to be done, should be done speedily; for, by Mr. Wyndham's account, we have no time to lose.

If we have the proper vessels, I am confident, the French will not be able to bring their ten thousand men by sea; and; should they attempt to pass through the Genoese territories, I hope the Austrians will prevent them: but, however, should all our precautions not be able to prevent the enemy's possessing themselves of Leghorn, yet we are not to despair. Fourteen days from their entry, if the allied powers unite heartily, I am confident, we shall take them all prisoners. I am confident, it can—and, therefore, should such an unlucky event take place, as their possessing themselves of Leghorn, I hope, will—be done. I have sent to the Admiral.

I am, very lately, from off Toulon; where thirteen sail of the line, and five frigates, are ready for sea, and others fitting.

With my best respects to Lady Hamilton, believe me, dear Sir, your
 Excellency's most obedient servant,

HORATIO NELSON.

III.

Vanguard, Syracuse, July 20th, 1798.

MY DEAR SIR,

It is an old saying, "The devil's children have the devil's luck." I cannot find—or, to this moment learn, beyond vague conjecture—where the French fleet are gone to. All my ill fortune, hitherto, has proceeded from want of frigates.

Off Cape Passaro, on the twenty-second of June, at day-light, I saw two frigates, which were supposed to be French; and it has been said, since, that a line-of-battle ship was to leeward of them, with the riches of Malta on board. But it was the destruction of the enemy, and not riches for myself, that I was seeking: these would have fell to me, if I had had frigates; but, except the ship of the line, I regard not all the riches in this world.

From my information off Malta, I believed they were gone to Egypt: therefore, on the twenty-eighth, I was communicating with Alexandria in Egypt; where I found the Turks preparing to resist them, but knew nothing beyond report.

From thence I stretched over to the coast of Caramania; where, not speaking a vessel who could give me information, I became distressed for the kingdom of the Two Sicilies: and, having gone a round of six hundred leagues, at this season of the year, (with a single ship, with an expedition incredible) here I am, as ignorant of the situation of the enemy as I was twenty-seven days ago!

I sincerely hope, the dispatches, which I understand are at Cape Passaro, will give me full information. I shall be able, for nine or ten weeks longer, to keep the fleet on active service, when we shall want provisions and stores. I send a paper on that subject, herewith.

Mr. Littledale is, I suppose, sent up by the Admiral to victual us, and I hope he will do it cheaper than any other person: but, if I find out that he charges more than the fair price, and has not the provisions of the very best quality, I will not take them; for, as no fleet has more fag than this, nothing but the best food, and greatest attention, can keep them healthy. At this moment, we have not one sick man in the fleet.

In about six days, I shall sail from hence: and, if I hear nothing more of the French, I shall go to the Archipelago; where, if they are gone towards Constantinople, I shall hear of them.

I shall go to Cyprus; and, if they are gone to Alexandretta, or any other part of Syria or Egypt, I shall get information.

You will, I am sure, and so will our country, easily conceive what has passed in my anxious mind; but I have this comfort, that I have no fault to accuse myself of: this bears me up, and this only.

I send you a paper, where a letter is fixed for different places: which I may leave at any place; and, except those who have the key, none can tell where I am gone to.

July 21.

The messenger is returned from Cape Passaro; and says, that your letters for me are returned to Naples. What a situation am I placed in! As yet, I can learn nothing of the enemy: therefore, I have no conjecture but that they are gone to Syria; and, at Cyprus, I hope to hear of them.

If they were gone to the westward, I rely that every place in Sicily would have information for me; for it is too important news to leave me in one moment's doubt about.

I have no frigate, or a sign of one. The masts, yards, &c. for the Vanguard, will I hope be prepared directly: for, should the French be so strongly secured in port that I cannot get at them, I shall immediately shift my flag into some other ship, and send the Vanguard to Naples to be refitted; for hardly any person but myself would have continued on service so long in such a wretched state.

I want to send a great number of papers to Lord St. Vincent; but I durst not trust any person here to carry them, even to Naples.

Pray, send a copy of my letter to Lord Spencer; he must be very anxious to hear of this fleet.

I have taken the liberty of troubling your Excellency with a letter for Lady Nelson. Pray, forward it for me; and believe me, with the greatest respect, your most obedient servant,

  HORATIO NELSON.

Sent on shore, to the charge of the Governor of Syracuse.

IV.

Vanguard, Syracuse, July 22d, 1798.

MY DEAR SIR,

I have had so much said about the King of Naples's orders only to admit three or four of the ships of our fleet into his ports, that I am astonished! I understood, that private orders, at least, would have been given for our free admission. If we are to be refused supplies, pray send me, by many vessels, an account, that I may in good time take the King's fleet to Gibraltar. Our treatment is scandalous, for a great nation to put up with; and the King's flag is insulted at every friendly port we look at.

I am, with the greatest respect, your most obedient servant,

HORATIO NELSON.

P.S. I do not complain of the want of attention in individuals, for all classes of people are remarkably attentive to us.

Sent on shore, to the charge of the Governor of Syracuse.

V.

Vanguard, Mouth of the Nile,
August 8th, 1798.

MY DEAR SIR,

Almighty God has made me the happy instrument in destroying the enemy's fleet; which, I hope, will be a blessing to Europe.

You will have the goodness to communicate this happy event to all the courts in Italy; for my head is so indifferent, that I can scarcely scrawl this letter.

Captain Capel, who is charged with my dispatches for England, will give you every information. Pray, put him in the quickest mode of getting home.

You will not send, by post, any particulars of this action, as I should be sorry to have any accounts get home before my dispatches.

I hope there will be no difficulty in our getting refitted at Naples. Culloden must be instantly hove down, and Vanguard all new masts and bowsprit. Not more than four or five sail of the line will probably come to Naples; the rest will go with the prizes to Gibraltar.

As this army never will return, I hope to hear the Emperor has regained the whole of Italy.

With every good wish, believe me, dear Sir, your most obliged and affectionate

HORATIO NELSON.

9th August.

I have intercepted all Buonaparte's dispatches going to France. This army is in a scrape, and will not get out of it.

VI.

August 12th, 1798.

MY DEAR SIR,

As the greater part of this squadron is going down the Mediterranean, we shall not want the quantity of wine or bread ordered; therefore, what is not already prepared had better be put a stop to. I will settle all the matter, if ever I live to see Naples.

I have the satisfaction to tell you, the French army have got a complaint amongst them—caused by the heat, and nothing but water—which will make Egypt the grave of the greatest part.

Ever your's, faithfully,

HORATIO NELSON.

VII.

Vanguard, off Malta;
October 24th, 1798.

MY DEAR SIR,

I am just arrived off this place; where I found Captain Ball, and the Marquis de Niza. From those officers, I do not find such an immediate prospect of getting possession of the town as the ministers at Naples seem to think. All the country, it is true, is in possession of the islanders; and, I believe, the French have not many luxuries in the town; but, as yet, their bullocks are not eat up.

The Marquis tells me, the islanders want arms, victuals, mortars, and cannon, to annoy the town. When I get the elect of the people on board, I shall desire them to draw up a memorial for the King of Naples, stating their wants and desires, which I shall bring with me.

The Marquis sails for Naples to-morrow morning. Till he is gone, I shall not do any thing about the island; but I will be fully master of that subject before I leave this place.

God bless you! is the sincere prayer of

HORATIO NELSON.

VIII.

Vanguard, off Malta,
October 27th, 1798.

MY DEAR SIR WILLIAM,

Although I believe I shall be at Naples before the cutter, yet I should be sorry to omit acknowledging your kind letter of the twenty-sixth.

When I come to Naples, I can have nothing pleasant to say of the conduct of his Sicilian Majesty's ministers towards the inhabitants of Malta, who wish to be under the dominion of their legitimate Sovereign. The total neglect and indifference with which they have been treated, appears to me cruel in the extreme.

Had not the English supplied fifteen hundred stand of arms, with bayonets, cartouch-boxes, and ammunition, &c. &c. and the Marquis supplied some few, and kept the spirit of those brave islanders from falling off, they must long ago have bowed again to the French yoke.

Could you, my dear Sir William, have believed, after what General Acton and the Marquis de Gallo had said, in our various conversations relative to this island, that nothing had been sent by the Governor of Syracuse—secretly (was the word to us) or openly—to this island? And, I am farther assured, that the Governor of Syracuse never had any orders sent him to supply the smallest article.

I beg your Excellency will state this, in confidence, to General Acton. I shall, most assuredly, tell it to the King! The justice I owe myself, now I feel employed in the service of their Sicilian Majesties, demands it of me; and, also, the duty I owe our gracious King, in order to shew that I am doing my utmost to comply with his royal commands.

As I have before stated, had it not been for the English, long, long ago, the Maltese must have been overpowered. Including the fifteen hundred stand of arms given by us, not more than three thousand are in the island. I wonder how they have kept on the defensive so long.

The Emerald will sail—in twenty-four hours after my arrival—for Malta; at least, two thousand stand of small arms complete, ammunition, &c. &c. should be sent by her. This is wanted, to defend themselves: for offence, two or three large mortars; fifteen hundred shells, with all necessaries; and, perhaps, a few artillery—two ten-inch howitzers, with a thousand shells. The Bormola, and all the left side of the harbour, with this assistance, will fall. Ten thousand men are required to defend those works, the French can only spare twelve hundred; therefore, a vigorous assault in many parts, some one must succeed.

But, who have the government of Naples sent to lead or encourage these people? A very good—and, I dare say, brave—old man; enervated, and shaking with the palsy. This is the sort of man that they have sent; without any supply, without even a promise of protection, and without his bringing any answer to the repeated respectful memorials of these people to their Sovereign.

I know, their Majesties must feel hurt, when they hear these truths. I may be thought presuming; but, I trust, General Acton will forgive an honest seaman for telling plain truths. As for the other minister, I do not understand him; we are different men! He has been bred in a court, and I in a rough element. But, I believe, my heart is as susceptible of the finer feelings as his, and as compassionate for the distress of those who look up to me for protection.

The officer sent here should have brought supplies, promises of protection, and an answer from the King to their memorials: he should have been a man of judgment, bravery, and activity. He should be the first to lead them to glory; and the last, when necessary, to retreat: the first to mount the walls of the Bormola, and never to quit it. This is the man to send. Such, many such, are to be found. If he succeeds, promise him rewards; my life for it, the business would soon be over.

God bless you! I am anxious to get this matter finished. I have sent Ball, this day, to summon Goza; if it resists, I shall send on shore, and batter down the castle.

Three vessels, loaded with bullocks, &c. for the garrison, were taken yesterday; from Tripoli ten more are coming, but we shall have them.

I had almost forgot to mention, that orders should be immediately given, that no quarantine should be laid on boats going to the coast of Sicily for corn. At present, as a matter of favour, they have fourteen days only. Yesterday, there was only four days bread in the island. Luckily, we got hold of a vessel loaded with wheat, and sent her into St. Paul's.

Once more, God bless you! and ever believe me, your obliged and affectionate

HORATIO NELSON.

This day, I have landed twenty barrels of gunpowder (two thousand eight hundred pounds) at Malta.

IX.

Palermo, January 10th, 1800.

SIR,

Your Excellency having had the goodness to communicate to me a dispatch from General Acton; together with several letters from Girganti, giving an account that a violence had been committed, in that port, by the seizing, and carrying off to Malta, two vessels loaded with corn—I beg leave to express to your Excellency my real concern, that even the appearance of the slightest disrespect should be offered, by any officers under my command, to the flag of his Sicilian Majesty: and I must request your Excellency to state fully to General Acton, that the act ought not to be considered as any intended disrespect to his Sicilian Majesty; but as an act of the most absolute and imperious necessity, either that the island of Malta should have been delivered up to the French, or that the King's orders should be anticipated for these vessels carrying their cargoes of corn to Malta.

I trust, that the government of this country will never again force any of our Royal Master's servants to so unpleasant an alternative.

I have the honour to be, with the greatest respect, your Excellency's most obedient and faithful servant,

B.N.

X.

March 8th, 1800.

MY DEAR SIR WILLIAM,

I thank you kindly for all your letters and good wishes. It is my determination, my health requiring it, to come to Palermo, and to stay two weeks with you.

I must again urge, that four gunb-oats may be ordered for the service of Malta; they will most essentially assist in the reduction of the place, by preventing small vessels from getting in or out.

I think, from the enemy, on the night of the fourth, trying and getting out for a short distance, a very fast-sailing polacca, that Vaubois is extremely anxious to send dispatches to France, to say he cannot much longer hold out: and, if our troops, as Captain Blackwood thinks, are coming from Gibraltar and Minorca, I have no idea the enemy will hold out a week.

I beg General Acton will order the gun-boats.

Troubridge has got the jaundice, and is very ill.

As I shall so very soon see you, I shall only say, that I am ever, your obliged and affectionate

BRONTE NELSON.

XI.

Palermo, March 30th, 1800.

MY DEAR SIR WILLIAM,

As, from the orders I have given, to all the ships under my command, to arrest and bring into port all the vessels and troops returning by convention with the Porte to France—and as the Russian ships have similar orders—I must request that your Excellency will endeavour to arrange with the government of this country, how in the first instance they are to be treated and received in the ports of the Two Sicilies: for, it is obvious, I can do nothing more than bring them into port; and, if they are kept on board ship, the fever will make such ravages as to be little short of the plague.

It is a very serious consideration for this country, either to receive them, or let them pass; when they would invade, probably, these kingdoms. In my present situation in the King's fleet, I have only to obey; had I been, as before, in the command, I should have gone one short and direct road to avert this great evil: viz. to have sent a letter to the French, and the Grand Vizir, in Egypt, that I would not, on any consideration, permit a single Frenchman to leave Egypt—and I would do it at the risk of even creating a coldness, for the moment, with the Turks.

Of two evils, choose the least; and nothing can be so horrid, as permitting that horde of thieves to return to Europe.

If all the wise heads had left them to God Almighty, after the bridge was broke, all would have ended well! For I differ entirely with my Commander in Chief, in wishing they were permitted to return to France; and, likewise, with Lord Elgin, in the great importance of removing them from

Egypt. No; there they should perish! has ever been the firm determination of your Excellency's most obedient and faithful servant,

BRONTE NELSON OF THE NILE.

XII.

Palermo, April 10th, 1800.

MY DEAR SIR WILLIAM,

Reports are brought to me, that the Spanish ships of war in this port are preparing to put to sea; a circumstance which must be productive of very unpleasant consequences, to both England and this country.

It is fully known, with what exactness I have adhered to the neutrality of this port; for, upon our arrival here, from Naples, in December 1798, from the conduct of his Catholic Majesty's minister, I should have been fully justified in seizing those ships.

We know, that one object of the Spanish fleet, combined with the French, was to wrest entirely from the hands of his Sicilian Majesty his kingdoms of the Two Sicilies.

The Spaniards are, by bad councils, the tools of the French; and, of course, the bitter enemy of his Sicilian Majesty and family.

The conduct I have pursued towards these ships, circumstanced as they are, has been moderate, and truly considerate towards his Sicilian Majesty.

The time is now come—that, profiting of my forbearance, the Spanish ships are fitting for sea. It is not possible, if they persist in their preparations, that I can avoid attacking them, even in the port of Palermo; for they never can, or shall, be suffered to go to sea, and placed in a situation of assisting the French, against not only Great Britain, but also the Two Sicilies.

I have, therefore, to request, that your Excellency will convey my sentiments on this very delicate subject to his Sicilian Majesty's ministers, that they may take measures to prevent such a truly unpleasant event happening; which would be as much against my wish as it can be against their's: and I request that your Excellency will, through its proper channel, assure his Sicilian Majesty, that his safety and honour is as dear to me as that of our Royal Master.

I have the honour to be, with the greatest respect, my dear Sir
 William, your Excellency's most affectionate, humble servant,

BRONTE NELSON OF THE NILE.

Letters FROM LORD NELSON TO MRS. THOMSON.

Letters OF LORD NELSON, &c.

I.

See LETTER X.

I sit down, my Dear Mrs. T. by desire of poor Thomson, to write you a line: not, to assure you of his eternal love and affection for you and his dear child; but only to say, that he is well, and as happy as he can be, separated from all which he holds dear in this world. He has no thoughts separated from your love, and your interest. They are united with his; one fate, one destiny, he assures me, awaits you both. What can I say more? Only, to kiss his child for him: and love him as truly, sincerely, and faithfully, as he does you; which is, from the bottom of his soul. He desires, that you will more and more attach yourself to dear Lady Hamilton.

II.

See LETTER XXXVI.

My Dearest Beloved * * * *,

To say, that I think of you by day, night, and all day, and all night, but too faintly express my feelings of love and affection towards you * * * * * * * * * unbounded affection. Our dear excellent, good * * * * * * * is the only one who knows any thing of the matter; and she has promised me, when you * * * * * * again, to take every possible care of you, as a proof of her never-failing regard for your own dear Nelson. Believe me, that I am incapable of wronging you, in thought, word, or deed. No; not all the wealth of Peru could buy me for one moment: it is all your's, and reserved wholly for you; and * * * certainly * * * * * * * * * from the first moment of our happy, dear, enchanting, blessed meeting. The thoughts of such happiness, my dearest only beloved, makes the blood fly into my head. The call of our country, is a duty which you would, deservedly, in the cool moments of reflection, reprobate, was I to abandon: and I should feel so disgraced, by seeing you ashamed of me! No longer saying—"This is the man who has saved his country! This is he who is the first to go forth to fight our battles, and the last to return!" And, then, all these honours reflect on you. "Ah!" they will think; "what a man! what sacrifices has he not made, to secure our homes and property; even the society and happy union with the finest and most accomplished woman in the world." As you love, how must you feel! My heart is with you, cherish it. I shall, my best beloved, return—if it pleases God—a victor; and it shall be my study to transmit an unsullied name. There is no desire of wealth, no ambition, that could keep me from all my soul holds dear. No; it is to save my country, my wife in the eye of God, and * will tell you that it is all right: and, then, only think of our happy meeting.

Ever, for ever, I am your's, only your's, even beyond this world,

 NELSON & BRONTE.

For ever, for ever, your own NELSON.

August 26th, [1803.]

Letters FROM LADY HAMILTON TO LORD NELSON.

Letters OF LADY HAMILTON, &c.

I.

Naples, June 30th, 1798.

DEAR SIR,

I take the opportunity of Captain Hope, to write a few lines to you, and thank you for your kind letter by Captain Bowen.

The Queen was much pleased, as I translated it for her: and charges me to thank you; and say, she prays for your honour and safety—victory, she is sure you will have.

We have still the regicide minister here, Garrat: the most impudent, insolent dog; making the most infamous demands every day; and I see plainly, the court of Naples must declare war, if they mean to save their country.

Her Majesty sees, and feels, all you said in your letter to Sir William, dated off the Faro di Messina, in its true light; so does General Acton.

But, alas! their First Minister, Gallo, is a frivolous, ignorant, self-conceited coxcomb, that thinks of nothing but his fine embroidered coat, ring, and snuff-box; and half Naples thinks him half a Frenchman: and, God knows, if one may judge of what he did in making the peace for the

Emperor, he must either be very ignorant, or not attached to his masters or the cause commune.

The Queen and Acton cannot bear him, and consequently [he] cannot have much power: but, still, a First Minister, although he may be a minister of smoke, yet he has always something; enough, at least, to do mischief.

The Jacobins have all been lately declared innocent, after suffering four years imprisonment; and, I know, they all deserved to be hanged long ago: and, since Garrat has been here, and through his insolent letters to Gallo, these pretty gentlemen, that had planned the death of their Majesties, are to be let out on society again.

In short, I am afraid, all is lost here; and I am grieved to the heart for our dear, charming Queen, who deserves a better fate!

I write to you, my dear Sir, in confidence, and in a hurry.

I hope you will not quit the Mediterranean, without taking us. We have our leave, and every thing ready, at a day's notice, to go: but yet, I trust in God, and you, that we shall destroy those monsters, before we go from hence. Surely, their reign cannot last long!

If you have any opportunity, write to us; pray, do: you do not know how your letters comfort us.

God bless you, my dear, dear Sir! and believe me, ever, your most sincerely obliged and attached friend,

EMMA HAMILTON.

II.

Thursday Evening, June 12th, [1799.]

I have been with the Queen this evening. She is very miserable; and says, that although the people of Naples are for them, in general, YET things will not be brought to that state of quietness and subordination, till the fleet of Lord Nelson appears off Naples. She therefore begs, intreats, and conjures you, my dear Lord, if it is possible, to arrange matters so as to be able to go to Naples.

Sir William is writing for General Acton's answer.

For God's sake, consider it, and do! We will go with you, if you will come and fetch us.

Sir William is ill; I am ill: it will do us good.

God bless you! Ever, ever, your's sincerely,

E. HAMILTON.

Letters FROM THE REV. EDMUND NELSON (Lord Nelson's Father) TO LADY HAMILTON.

Letters OF THE REV. EDMUND NELSON, &c.

I.

Madam,

I am much favoured by your polite letter, and the very friendly regard with which Sir William Hamilton and yourself always mention my dear son; who is, certainly, a worthy, good, brave man, parental partiality apart. But, I myself am by no means satisfied with his present situation; as to its importance, its safety, or its merited rewards. It [is] his to sow, but others reap the yellow harvests. All things, I trust, however, will work together for good.

Captain Parker's misfortune, I see, in every point of view, with a friendly concern. Langford will quickly be upon his legs.

Though the amusements of a dirty sea-port are not the most refined, good health, and domestic cheerfulness, will be a happy substitute.

I beg the whole party to accept this my remembrance; and assurance of my regard, respect, and love: and am, Madam, your most humble servant,

EDM. NELSON.

Burnham, August 11th, [1801.]

II.

Madam,

Your polite congratulation upon the entrance of a new year, I return seven-fold to you, and the whole of the party now under the hospitable roof of Merton Place. Time is a sacred deposit committed to our trust; and, hereafter, we must account for the use we have made of it. To me, a large portion of this treasure has already been granted, even seventy-nine years. The complaint my dear son has felt is, I know, very, very painful: and can be removed, only, with much care and caution; not venturing, without a thick covering, both head and feet, even to admire your parterres of snow-drops, which now appear in all their splendour. The white robe which January wears, bespangled with ice, is handsome to look at; but we must not approach too near her.

I shall be very glad to know the Lord of Merton is recovered.

I am, Madam, your most humble servant,

EDM. NELSON.

Bath, January 7th, 1802.

Letters From The REV. DR. NELSON, NOW EARL NELSON, TO LADY HAMILTON.

Letters OF EARL NELSON, &c.

I.

Hilborough, near Brandon,
Wednesday, March 4th, 1801.

My Dear Lady,

I have sent you, by this day's coach, a hunted hare; which, I hope, will prove tender and good. It was killed yesterday.

We are very much gratified by your kind and friendly letters: they are very interesting to us, and they give an additional zest to our breakfast; indeed, they are the only things give us any comfort, in our absence. How unfortunate it was, we left town as we did! I had a letter, yesterday morning, from my great and beloved Brother. He tells me, he has sent my letter to the new Lord Chancellor; God grant it may have the desired effect; but, they are all so engaged, that I fear it much. At any rate, our good Friend has done what he can. He tells me, he shall be at Yarmouth to-morrow or next day. A near relation of our's, who has not seen my Lord since his return to England, has offered to take me in his carriage: so, we set out on Sunday afternoon; for we parsons can't go till the Sunday duty is over. We sleep at Norwich, and hope to be at Yarmouth early on Monday.

I have written to my Brother by this post; so that, if he is likely to have sailed before Monday, he has time to stop us. Yarmouth is sixty miles from hence.

I have written you all these particulars; because, I know, you like to know all about us.

Mrs. Nelson does not go with us; so you must be charitable to her, and give her a letter or two. We shall return by the following Sunday.

I see, by the papers, the King was better on Tuesday.

Mrs. Nelson is going out for a day; when she returns, she will write. She will thank you to keep the two guineas my Lord left for Charlotte, till you hear from her; as she has thought of laying it out in a frock for her.

We both join in united regards to Sir William; and believe me, your
 Ladyship's faithful and most obliged and affectionate friend,

Wm. NELSON.

II.

Hilborough, March 29th, 1801.

My Dear Lady,

As I have duty to-day, both morning and afternoon, and to preach twice, I have only time to scrawl a few lines to you between the services. I will write to my deary to-morrow.

I do not much wonder we have no news from the Baltic, considering the state of the wind; and, unless it changes, it may be some time first. Pray God it may be good, when it does arrive.

I was rather surprised to hear Tom Tit (that bad bird) had taken his flight to town: but, he is a prying little animal, and wishes to know every thing; and, as he is so small and insignificant, his movements are not always observed. But, for God's sake, take care of him; and caution our little jewel to be as much upon her guard as she can. I am terribly afraid, this bird will endeavour to do mischief. He must be watched with a hawk's eye. I almost wish some hawk, or Jove's eagle, would either devour him or frighten him away.

It is not very likely I should hear from Yarmouth before you, because our Yarmouth letters generally go to London first; but if I should, accidentally, your Ladyship shall depend on hearing from me immediately.

I am glad my little Horace looks so well; and that you think him so like his great, his glorious, his immortal Uncle. Why should he not be like him? Is it so very uncommon for such near relations to have some similitude? They who say otherwise, only say it out of envy, malice and hatred, and all uncharitableness; out upon all such miscreants! say I.

My love to deary, Charlotte, and the hereditary Duke of Bronte.

God bless you, my dear Lady; and believe me, your's faithfully,

Wm. NELSON.

Tell me, in your next, whether you have seen that little bird, called Tom Tit.

III.

Hilborough, August 23d, 1801.

MY DEAR LADY HAMILTON,

I have written two long letters to my jewel, but I still seem to have more to say. I can't find out whether a certain Viscountess is expected at Burnham, or no.

I am pleased that you propose bringing Mrs. Nelson to Hilborough. I hope, Sir William will be able to amuse himself with fishing a little. The weather is too hot for me to come to London, and I can't leave my parish at this time.

Tell my Brother, I should have great pleasure in seeing him; and will go with him to Plymouth, or any where else, if he particularly desires it. When you have seen Parker and Langford, you can give me a particular account of the state of their wounds. I feel much for them. I think it is better the Cub did not speak to Mrs. N. It will save some trouble.

I wish you could get a comfortable house near London.

You will find Mr. Nayler, of the Herald's Office, a pleasant young man. I believe, he is my friend, and will readily give every information in his power.

If Jove gets a higher title, perhaps things may be settled more to our minds. Now we are already in the patent, as Barons; it will be no difficult matter, in that case, to have our entails advanced to the highest honour, if my brother wishes.

This I only mention entre nous, without having a desire on the subject. I am perfectly satisfied, that I am in the patent. I don't mean to say more to my Brother.

I am told, there are two or three very old lives, Prebends of Canterbury, in the Minister's gift—near six hundred pounds a year, and good houses.

The Deans of Hereford, Exeter, Litchfield and Coventry, York, and Winchester, are old men.

Write from Deal, and tell me when you are likely to return to London.

You can't come from thence nearer than London, unless my Brother lands you on the other side of the river Thames, on the Essex or Suffolk coasts. If that plan takes place, Mrs. Nelson had better send Sarah home before you go.

Compliments to Sir William, and all friends. Your's very faithfully,

Wm. NELSON.

IV.

Sunday Morning, Sept. 6th, [1801.]

My Dear Lady,

To be sure, you did promise to write to me on Thursday last; and I was very much disappointed at not receiving a letter yesterday, and sent to the Post Office twice, to be certain there was no mistake: and, now, this morning, comes your roguish, waggish letter, on a Sunday morning, (amidst all my meditations for the good of my parishioners) about love, courtship, marriage, throwing the stocking, going to bed, &c. &c. &c.—quite shocking to write to a country parson, who can have no idea of such things. It might do well enough for a King's chaplain; or a church dignitary, who is supposed to have more learning, and more knowledge of things in general.

I wish you was here, and you should not laugh at me for nothing. I would give you as good as you brought, at any time.

I'll have no Emmas, at present. Stay till there comes one or two of another sort, to keep the line of the Nelsons in the true name and blood, without being obliged to go to others to assume a name which scarcely belongs to them; and, then, as many Emmas, Elfridas, Evelindas, and Evelinas, as you please.

But, I hope to God, the present young Horatio will go on as we all wish, and transmit a long race to posterity.

I am delighted with Dr. Heath's letter to my Brother, and the character he gives of him. My only fear is, that we shall spoil him among us.

I have not yet heard from him, how he felt himself. I should have liked to have peeped slyly into his room, and seen how he acted on first receiving the joyful intelligence.

I don't know enough how to thank my Brother, for all his goodness to me and mine; my heart overflows, whenever I think of it: but I can't sit down, and write a formal letter of thanks; it would be too absurd for me to write, or him to read. He well knows me; and I leave it to your Ladyship, (my best and truest friend) to say every thing to him, for and from me: it will come best from your lips, and adorned with your eloquence.

I wish my Brother had done with this business. I hope, a peace will soon put an end to his toils and dangers. * * * *
* *

V.

Hilborough, September 8th, 1801.

MY DEAR LADY HAMILTON,

I hope you will have received my long letter of Sunday's date, by this time. I wonder you should accuse me of remissness, in not writing to you. I told you then, and I repeat it now, that I would always give you "as good as you brought:" and, upon looking back to the last week's letters, I find I have always answered your's, whenever I had one; and, generally, by the same post.

As I wrote so much on Sunday, and you said—you thought you should leave Deal on Tuesday or Wednesday, I said—I should write no more till you got back to London. Nor should I now, was it not to rebut the charge of remissness and inattention to you.

I am glad Mrs. Nelson is likely to come home soon; but, I hear nothing about your intentions. I shall write to her to-morrow, and direct my letter to Piccadilly; where, I hope, it will find her: and, if this letter travels to Deal, and follows you to London, it is no matter; it is not worth having, when you get it. Only, I could not bear the thoughts of the appearance of neglect, without deserving it.

One or two letters I wrote to Mrs. Nelson last week, I gave public notice, were intended, in a great degree, for the whole party.

Mrs. Bolton is here for a day, to help my solitary life. I find Lady N. has taken a house in Somerset Street, Portman Square. She, and my Father, are to spend the winter in

London; and, I am informed, he is to pay half. Whether it is ready-furnished, or not, I can't tell.

Mr. Edwards is this moment gone, and begs his compliments to you all.

Believe me, your's most faithfully,

 Wm. NELSON.

Compliments to Parker and Langford.

VI.

Canterbury, February 9th, 1805.

Dear Lady Hamilton,

I send you a small parcel; which I will thank you to forward to my Brother, if you think there is a chance of his getting it before he leaves the Mediterranean. But, if you have reason to expect him home very soon, you will be kind enough to return it to me again; or, keep it till I see you.

The ceremony of electing the new Archbishop takes place on Tuesday morning. I think it more than probable, we shall make choice of the person his Majesty has recommended to us, in his letter, which the Chapter received yesterday.

Mrs. Nelson begs her love to you, Charlotte, Mrs. Bolton, &c. &c.

Your's, very faithfully,

Wm. NELSON.

I received Mrs. Bolton's parcel safe on Friday.

Letters FROM THE EARL OF ST. VINCENT TO LADY HAMILTON.

Letters OF THE EARL OF ST. VINCENT, &c.

I.

My Dear Madam,

The prodigies of valour performed by your new Chevalier have, I fear, obliterated the memory of your ancient Knight. Nevertheless, I beg your Ladyship will lay me at the feet of the Queen of the Two Sicilies, and assure her Majesty of my profound respect for her person, and that my life is devoted to the defence of it: and, for yourself, accept every kind wish of your Ladyship's truly affectionate and faithful Knight,

ST. VINCENT.

Gibraltar, 18th October 1798.

II.

MY DEAR LADY HAMILTON,

Ten thousand most grateful thanks are due to your Ladyship, for restoring the health of our invaluable friend Nelson, on whose life the fate of the remaining governments in Europe, whose system has not been deranged by these devils, depends. Pray, do not let your fascinating Neapolitan dames approach too near him; for he is made of flesh and blood, and cannot resist their temptations.

Lady St. Vincent will be transported with your attention to her. I have sent the fan mounts for Lady Nelson and her, by Sir James Saumarez; who, after seeing the French prizes safe moored in the Tagus, conveys the Duke d'Hervie. He, poor man! although a Grandee of Spain, having been driven out of that kingdom by the insolent intrigues of Truguet.

I have obeyed your Ladyship's commands respecting Tom Bowen, who is now Captain of L'Aquilon, and gone to Lisbon to take possession of her; and his brother William, who married a daughter of Sir William Parker, I have appointed to the Caroline, the finest frigate I have, and he is employed on the most advantageous service for filling his pockets. Should your Ladyship have any other protegé, I desire you will not spare me.

I am very much penetrated with the condescension their Majesties of the Two Sicilies have graciously shewn to me, through your Ladyship, and I rely on your doing justice to my feelings upon the occasion.

I have taken up my residence here for some months, that I may be ready to afford succour to the detachments of the fleet I have the honour to command, in the Levant and before Cadiz; and, when Sir William and you arrive, I shall be able to give you some English mutton, in a plain way.

Continue to love me; and rest assured of the most unfeigned and affectionate regard of, my dear Lady Hamilton, your faithful and devoted Knight,

ST. VINCENT.

Admiral's House, Rosia, Gibraltar, 28th October 1798.

III.

MY DEAR LADY HAMILTON,

I have to thank you, which I do most kindly, for your obliging letters of the 7th and 10th of November; and for the gracious letter which your Ladyship had received from the charming, delightful Queen of the Two Sicilies, at whose feet I am anxiously desirous to throw myself: and, as I have relinquished my intention of returning to England, (although in possession of leave to go) I hope the period is not far distant. In the meanwhile, have the goodness to keep me alive in the remembrance of her Majesty: assure her of my profound respect and admiration for her as Queen—I dare not give utterance to what I feel for her as one of the first and most lovely of her sex.

Our possession of the island of Minorca will relieve her Majesty, and the government, from one embarrassment, touching their last treaty with France; as Lord Nelson will now be able to refit his squadron, without committing an infraction of the treaty.

Our excellent friend, General O'Hara, is very busy in erecting two rooms for the accommodation of your Ladyship and Sir William, when you visit this curious rock. He is among the most hospitable and entertaining of men: and we live together as all commanders of his Majesty's land forces and fleets ought to do; and, I hope, will do, from the examples which have been shewn wherever I have acted with the army—as Sir Charles Grey, the Governor of this garrison, and General Stuart, will testify; and, if the immortal Wolfe could be conjured from the grave, he would do so too.

I hope soon to hear, our dear Lord Nelson is quite well, under your fostering care; and, with my warmest wishes for every blessing to be showered down upon you and your's, I have the honour to be, with the truest respect, esteem, and regard, your Ladyship's very affectionate, humble servant,

ST. VINCENT.

Rosia House, Gibraltar, 7th Dec. 1798.

IV.

MY DEAR LADY HAMILTON,

Permit me to introduce to your acquaintance and protection another hero of the Nile, in Captain Darby, of the Bellerophon; who you will find a pleasant, queer, and faithful Irishman.

I also beg leave to interest you in favour of Mrs. Lock; a daughter of the Duchess of Leinster, by Mr. Ogilvie. Her husband is appointed Consul at Naples; which may occasion some difficulty in bringing her forward, unless the etiquette is altered touching Consuls.

God bless you, my dear Madam; and, be assured, I always am your
 Ladyship's truly affectionate

ST. VINCENT.

Rosia House, Gibraltar, 1st January 1799.

V.

MY DEAR LADY HAMILTON,

I cannot sufficiently thank you, for sending me her Sicilian Majesty's most gracious letter; the contents of which I feel, as becomes a good royalist, and loyal subject: and for your goodness to Mrs. Lock; who, poor thing! merits a more respectable situation than that of Consuless. She is, certainly, a very comely woman, and truly amiable.

The designation Sir William has in contemplation for him, will place them in an honourable stile; and, I have no doubt, from the protection they have at home, will lead to ministerial character.

You are very good to my old friend Darby—who is a good-humoured, blundering Irishman; and will make you laugh, in the midst of the pangs your Ladyship must suffer for the destiny of the delightful city and country to which you have so long contributed a large portion of the gaiety and charming society of Sir William's hospitable mansion: for, although I had not the good fortune to revisit Naples after Sir William's return, all my travelling friends did ample justice to the liberality of the representatives of our Royal Master and Mistress. Mr. Preston was chargé, when I was at Naples with the Duke of Gloucester; and, though a worthy gentleman, and since a pious Bishop, he was certainly a dry comedian.

Have the goodness to commend me to the Queen; continue to nurse my excellent friend, Nelson; and, when I have the happiness to see Sir William and your Ladyship here, I will pour the effusions of my heart upon you both. The Governor has added two rooms to the convent, for your accommodation; and Mrs. Grey, late Miss Whitbread, wife to the Captain of the Ville de Paris, will contribute all that this house affords for the entertainment of both.

God bless you, my dear Lady Hamilton; and, be assured, no man respects and esteems you more truly than your Ladyship's truly affectionate

ST. VINCENT.

Rosia House, 27th February 1799.

Letters FROM SIR ALEXANDER JOHN BALL TO LADY HAMILTON.

Letters OF SIR ALEXANDER JOHN BALL, &c.

I.

My Dear Madam,

I cannot help loving and esteeming you very much, although you have proved such a false gipsey to me. Pray, do you recollect looking into my hand, and telling me a pretty story of carrying home Sir William and Lady Hamilton, &c. &c. However, I forgive you; as you did not take money, and could only have in view giving me much pleasure.

I beg leave to introduce to your Ladyship's notice the Abbé Savoye; who is a sensible man, and the most polished here. He has great influence with the Maltese. Pray, request Sir William to introduce him particularly to Le Chevalier Acton.

I shall have the pleasure of seeing you and Sir William Hamilton in England, this summer. How very much I wished to be near you, when you were reading the parliamentary effusions of gratitude and joy for the services Lord Nelson has rendered his country! I would rather be Lord Nelson, than any Duke—or, indeed, any man—in England; and you may guess how very proud I am in having such a friend. Indeed, I feel, that I owe more to him than any man in this world. I have written to Sir William; God bless you both!

I remain, with sincere respect and esteem, my dear Madam, your Ladyship's most devoted and obliged humble servant,

ALEXANDER JOHN BALL.

Alexander, 9th February 1799.

Davidge Gould is sighing for Palermo; alias Miss K——. I wish the Admiral would let him recreate for a fortnight, and send Hardy to me again.

II.

My Dear Madam,

I had the honour of writing to your Ladyship and Sir William, by the Vanguard; since which, I have read the few lines you had the goodness to address to me at the bottom of Lord Nelson's letter of the 9th inst.

I cannot entertain any hopes of personally paying my respects to you and Sir William, before your departure for England; but, be assured, that I can never forget the very flattering attention you have both been pleased to honour me with.

You must wait a month longer, for the warm weather; otherwise, the transition may be too great for Sir William.

We are anxiously waiting for the Maltese deputies to return from Palermo. The inhabitants are critically situated; but, I hope, all will end well. Good news from you will determine it.

I find, that you fascinate all the navy as much at Palermo as you did at Naples. If we had many such advocates, every body would be a candidate for our profession.

God bless, and protect, you and Sir William. May prosperous gales attend you! May you live a thousand years!
Believe me, with sincere respect and esteem, my dear Madam, your Ladyship's most devoted and obliged servant,

ALEXANDER JOHN BALL.

23d February 1799.

Letters FROM THE EARL OF BRISTOL, Bishop of Derry, in Ireland, TO LADY HAMILTON.

Letters OF THE EARL OF BRISTOL, Bishop of Derry, &c.

I.

Naples, Sunday Morning, [1795.]

I return you the inclosed, my Dearest Emma, which does equal honour to the excellent head and heart of the writer. I shall begin, for the first time of my life, to have a good opinion of myself, after such honourable testimonials.

In the mean time, I send you an extraordinary piece of news, just written me from Ratisbon—a courier from the Elector of Mentz, desiring the Empire to make a separate peace with France.

Couriers have been sent from the Diet to Sweden and Denmark, desiring their mediation: "and it is clear," says my letter, "Somebody is at the bottom of all this; the Elector of Mentz only lends his name."

The suburbs of Warsaw taken; the capitulation of the city daily expected.

The King of Prussia totally retired beyond Potsdam, and supposed to be at the eve of madness.

  Oh! Emma, who'd ever be wise,
   If madness be loving of thee.

B.

II.

Munich, 14th July 1795.

Dearest Emma,

Here is great news from England. My letters of the 26th June assure me, seven thousand men are embarked for St. Pol de Leon, together with an immense number of emigrés—that, the week before, a bishop, and sixty priests, were most prosperously landed at the same place, and received with the greatest acclamations—that six sail of the line from Russia, were in sight, and the pilots gone to conduct them—that, in Amsterdam, and other towns of Holland, there is the greatest insurrections in favour of that fool the Stadtholder. All this, however, can only tend to facilitate peace, but not at all to restore that despicable, odious family of Bourbons—the head of which is now at Verona, where we left him eating two capons a day; ('tis a pity the whole family are not capons!) and, what is more, dressing them himself in a superb kitchen—the true chapel of a Bourbon Prince.

Emma! if that dear Queen of Naples does not write, herself, to Prince D'Oria, for me, I won't look at your beautiful face these six months—"coute qui coute."

To-morrow, for Pyrmont, near Hanover. Emma—adieu!

III.

There is no doubt but Don Luizi is implicated: that very circumstance, argues the extent of the mischief; for so cautious a man, and one whose sentiments are so publicly known, would not engage without good support.

I have conversed with one of his intimates—one "who is no stranger to his dearest secret." The evidence will be difficult; perhaps, impracticable: unless his most confidential friends can be gained; and that, I deem, impossible.

But the character of the Garrison at Capua is of the most alarming complexion; and, yet, is what I can best depend on. I think, Wade could tell much, if he would speak out.

Adieu!

Lovel and I were on Vesuvius. He goes, like a true parson, only to eat the better. I foresee, he will once more fall into Nudi's hands. Procyta will be another Duo; for I hate large parties on such, and especially females—unless they be Phoenixes, like yourself.

It is a great discouragement to a Caserta party, to view the whole town buried in a mist; and the Belvidere alone, like a buoy, to point out the shoal.

Sweet Emma—adieu!

Every wish of my heart beats for the dear Queen.

IV.

Send me word, Dearest Emma! how the invaluable, adorable Queen, finds herself.

The weather changed so unmercifully, yesterday, that Lovel and I both grew ill; and this makes me the more anxious to hear of our too sensible and inestimable Queen. My warmest wishes—physical, political, and moral—ever attend her.

B.

V.

Here is my cousin's answer, Dearest Emma—"Io lo capisco." Her brother assured me, there is not the semblance of an insurrection; and, that our dear, dear Queen, is misled by a set of scoundrels.

Send me word where you will be. Adieu!

VI.

Yesterday, we dined on Mount Vesuvius; to-day, we were to have dined on its victim, Pompeii: but, "by the grace of God, which passeth all understanding," since Bartolomeo himself, that weather-soothsayer, did not foresee this British weather, we are prevented.

In the mean time, all this week and the next, is replete with projects to Ischia, Procita, &c. &c. so God only knows when I can worship, again, my Diana of Ephesus.

Write me word, explicitly, how you are, what you are, and where you are; and be sure that, wheresoever I am, still I am your's, my dearest Emma.

VII.

Wednesday.

MY DEAREST EMMA,

The very unexpected intelligence, which Prince Augustus has most delicately communicated to me, of poor Lord Hervey's decease, has quite bouleversée my already shattered frame.

I would not allow your friendly mind to learn an event so interesting to me from any other hand than that of your affectionate and devoted friend,

BRISTOL.

VIII.

MY EVER DEAREST LADY HAMILTON,

I should certainly have made this Sunday an holy day to me, and have taken a Sabbath day's journey to Caserta, had not poor Mr. Lovel been confined to his bed above three days with a fever.

To-day, it is departed; to-morrow, Dr. Nudi has secured us from its resurrection; and, after to-morrow, I hope, virtue will be its own reward, and that my friendship for Lovel will be recompensed with the enjoyment.

This moment I receive your billet-doux, and very dulcet it is!

All public and private accounts agree, in the immediate prospect of a general peace. It will make a delicious foreground in the picture of the new year; many of which, I wish, from the top, bottom, and centre of my heart, to the incomparable Emma—quella senza paragona!

Dans ce moment, on m'assure que Mayence est prise. Je ne vous garantis pas cette maudite nouvelle—mais je me flatte que la paix se fait.

IX.

EVER DEAREST EMMA,

I went down to your Opera box two minutes after you left it; and should have seen you on the morning of your departure—but was detained in the arms of Murphy, as Lady Eden expressed it, and was too late.

You say nothing of the adorable Queen; I hope, she has not forgot me: but, as Shakespeare says, "Who doats, must doubt;" and I verily deem her the very best edition of a woman I ever saw—I mean; of such as are not in folio, and are to be had in sheets.

I will come on Friday or Saturday; but our British colony are so numerous, that my duties obstruct my pleasures.

Ever, and invariably, dearest, dear Emma, most affectionately, your

B.

You see, I am but the second letter of your alphabet, though you are the first of mine.

X.

Milan, 24th November 1798.

I know not, Dearest Emma, whether friend Sir William has been able to obtain my passport, or not; but this I know—that, if they have refused it, they are damned fools for their pains: for, never was a Malta orange better worth squeezing or sucking; and if they leave me to die, without a tombstone over me, to tell the contents—"tant pis pour eux!"

In the mean time, I will frankly confess to you, that my health most seriously and urgently requires the balmy air of dear Naples, and the more balmy atmosphere of those I love, and who love me; and that I shall forego my garret with more regret than most people of my silly rank in society forego a palace or a drawing-room.

But I will augur better things from the justice of my neighbour; and that they will not condemn, against all rules of probability, one of their best friends, unheard: especially, one who, if he be heard, can say so much.

My project, then, in case I receive the passport, is to travel on horseback as far as Spalato in Dalmatia; and, from thence, cross over to Manfredonia—a passage of a few hours—and which, in the year 1772, I performed with my horses on board; and, afterwards, had a most delightful jaunt through that unexplored region, Dalmatia; where the very first object that strikes both the eye and the imagination, is a modern city built within the precincts of an ancient palace—for Spalato stands within the innermost walls of Diocletian's palace. For that wise Sovereign quitted the sceptre for the pleasures of an architect's rule; and, when he had completed his mansion in that delightful climate, enjoyed that, and life, to a most advanced old age—

"The world forgetting, by the world forgot."

A-propos to Spalato! Do not fail hinting to Sir William, that a most safe, convenient, and expeditious packet-boat, might be established, in these perilous times, between that and Manfredonia: by which all dispatches, and all travellers, either for business or pleasure, might make a very short and safe cut between Naples and Vienna, and Naples and the rest of Europe, without touching one palm of any ground but Austrian and Neapolitan; and, of course, without the risk of being ever stopped.

The small towns, too, are in quick succession; and, the whole country being a limestone rock, the roads will make themselves, and afterwards pay themselves, by means of good turnpikes.

Nothing can exceed the dreariness, gloominess, and humidity, of a Milanese sky in winter; which, I conclude, under the old regime, led to all the hospitality, and conviviality, practised here, by their voluptuous but social nobility.

Now, we have nothing left to comfort, but another Nudi—a son of Esculapius, born in Italy; but an enthusiast for England, and all that is English—an excellent physician, but a still better friend; and, like Nudi, when he has a pint of Madeira in his belly, and the fumes of it in his brain, a most cheerful and improving companion: for, I protest to you that, during my convalescence, I made greater strides to recovery by his Attic evenings, than by his morning potions, or even his beef broth.

Sweet Emma, adieu! Remember me in the warmest and most enthusiastic stile, to your friend, and my friend, and the friend of human kind.

If Sir William does not contrive to send me my passport, I will—I will—excommunicate him, and send him to the devil before his time.

Letter FROM THE HONOURABLE CHARLES GREVILLE, Nephew of Sir William Hamilton, TO LADY HAMILTON.

Letter OF THE HONOURABLE CHARLES GREVILLE, &c.

August 18th, 1794.

DEAR LADY HAMILTON,

You will, I am sure, be glad to hear, that a favourable change has been announced to me; and that I am reinstated in the King's household, and honoured with a gold key, as his Vice-Chamberlain—and I hope, in a few days, to be in parliament.

You have seen me in prosperity, and in adversity; and know how much I estimate worldly concerns, according to their influencing the opinion of my real friends. Friendship has borne me up in the most difficult times; and the general satisfaction which my friends express, on my promotion, renders me very happy at present: and, to make me more so, I have anticipated to my own mind the sincere satisfaction with which you will receive this news.

I should not flatter myself so far, if I was not very sincerely interested in your happiness; and, ever, affectionately your's,

C.F.G.

Letters

FROM LADY HAMILTON TO THE HON. CHARLES GREVILLE, Nephew of Sir William Hamilton.

Letters OF LADY HAMILTON, &c.

I.

25th of February, [1800.]

DEAR SIR,

I received your letter by Mr. Campbell. He is lodged with us. We find him a pleasant man; and shall write fully by him. He will tell you a little how we go on, as to our domestic happiness. We are more united and comfortable than ever, in spite of the infamous Jacobin papers, jealous of Lord Nelson's glory, and Sir William's and mine. But we do not mind them. Lord N. is a truly virtuous and great man; and, because we have been fagging, and ruining our health, and sacrificing every comfort, in the cause of loyalty, our private characters are to be stabbed in the dark. First, it was said, Sir W. and Lord N. fought; then, that we played, and lost. First, Sir W. and Lord N. live like brothers; next, Lord N. never plays: and this I give you my word of honour. So I beg you will contradict any of these vile reports. Not that Sir W. and Lord N. mind it; and I get scolded by the Queen, and all of them, for having suffered one day's uneasiness.

Our fleet is off Malta: Lord Nelson has taken Le Genereux, and was after the frigates; so the attempt to relieve Malta has failed.

I have had a letter from the Emperor of Russia, with the Cross of Malta. Sir William has sent his Imperial Majesty's letter to Lord Grenville, to get me the permission to wear it. I have rendered some services to the poor Maltese. I got them ten thousand pounds, and sent corn when they were in distress. The deputies have been lodged in my house; I have been their Ambassadress, so his [I.]M. has rewarded me. If the King will give me leave to wear it abroad, it is of use to me. The Q——n is having the order set in diamonds for me; but the one the Emperor sent is gold. I tell you this little history of it, that you may be au fait. Ball has it also, but I am the first Englishwoman that ever had it. Sir W. is pleased, so I am happy. We are coming home; and I am miserable, to leave my dearest friend, the Q——. She cannot be consoled. We have sworn to be back in six months; and I will not quit her, till Sir William binds himself to come back. However, I shall have a comfort in seeing some of my old friends; and you, in particular. We have also many things to settle. I think, I can situate the person you mention about the Court, as a Camerist to some of the R. F——y, if her education is good.

It is a comfortable situation for life; so, I will bring her out.
The Q. has promised me. Let this remain entre nous.

II.

[April 1803.]

Lady Hamilton will be glad to know how long Mr. Greville can permit her to remain in the house in Piccadilly, as she must instantly look out for a lodging; and, therefore, it is right for her to know the full extent of time she can remain there. She also begs to know, if he will pay her debts, and what she may depend upon; that she may reduce her expences and establishment immediately.

END OF VOL. I.

Printed in Great Britain
by Amazon